Unleashing Financial Freedom

By

Lydiah Tate

Contents

Dedication

To The Almighty God, whose wisdom, grace, and unfailing love have been my guiding light throughout my journey. Without Your strength and divine purpose, this book would not have been possible.

To my beloved parents, Jane and Sam Wanyanga, for instilling in me the values of perseverance, integrity, and hard work. Your love and sacrifices have shaped me into the person I am today, and I am forever grateful.

To my wonderful children, Shahid, Asha, and Tariq Tate, who inspire me every day with their love, patience, and unwavering support. You are my greatest motivation, and I dedicate this work to your futures filled with wisdom, success, and financial empowerment.

To my church community and the immigrant communities across the nation, who have welcomed me and allowed me to share the principles of financial freedom. Your eagerness to learn and transform your lives continues to fuel my passion for financial education.

To my friends, family, and colleagues who have believed in me, encouraged me, and supported me through this journey. Your trust and faith have been my pillars of strength.

This book is dedicated to all those seeking financial independence and a life of abundance. May you find inspiration, knowledge, and the courage to take control of your financial future.

Acknowledgments

First and foremost, I give all honor and gratitude to The Almighty God, whose grace, wisdom, and divine guidance have been the foundation of my journey. Without His strength and provision, this book, *Unleashing Financial Freedom*, would not have been possible. He has given me the vision, resilience, and the ability to share this knowledge, and for that, I am eternally thankful.

To my beloved parents, Jane and Sam Wanyanga, your unwavering love, encouragement, and support have shaped me into the person I am today. You instilled in me the values of hard work, discipline, and integrity, which have been invaluable throughout my career and in writing this book. Your sacrifices and belief in my potential have fueled my determination to make a difference in the lives of others.

To my wonderful children, Shahid, Asha, and Tariq Tate, you are my greatest blessings and inspiration. Your love and patience during the long hours I spent writing and researching mean the world to me. You have been my motivation to push forward, knowing that the lessons in this book will not only empower others but also serve as a foundation for your own financial journeys. Thank you for your understanding and unwavering belief in me.

To my church community, thank you for providing me with a platform to teach and share the principles of financial freedom nationwide. Your support, prayers, and enthusiasm have encouraged me to extend my reach and empower individuals to take control of their financial destinies. The opportunities afforded to me through this community have been instrumental in refining my approach to financial education and making this book a reality.

To the many roles and experiences I have had in the financial industry over the years, each challenge and opportunity has contributed to the depth of knowledge I share in this book. From working with clients to navigating the intricacies of financial systems, every experience has strengthened my passion for helping others achieve financial independence. The lessons learned along the way have provided invaluable insights that have shaped the content of *Unleashing Financial Freedom*.

To my friends and family all over the world, your trust, encouragement, and unwavering support have meant everything to me. You have been my sounding board, my cheerleaders, and my greatest allies. Whether through words of encouragement, feedback on my ideas, or simply believing in my vision, you have played an essential role in bringing this book to life. Your faith in me has been a driving force, and for that, I am deeply grateful.

To my readers, I extend my deepest gratitude. You are the reason this book exists, and it is my sincere hope that *Unleashing Financial Freedom* will inspire, educate, and empower you on your financial journey. Whether you are just beginning to take control of your finances or looking for ways to build lasting wealth, this book is designed to provide practical strategies and transformative insights. Your willingness to learn, grow, and take action will make all the difference in your financial future. Thank you for trusting me as your guide, and I hope this book serves as a valuable resource in your pursuit of true financial freedom.

This book is a testament to the collective support, love, and wisdom of all these incredible people in my life. I am humbled and honored to share *Unleashing Financial Freedom* with the world, and I dedicate its success to each of you who have played a part in this journey. Thank you from the depths of my heart.

About the Author

Lydiah Tate is a seasoned financial expert with over 30 years of experience in the banking and financial services industry. She holds a Bachelor's degree in Finance and an MBA, which have provided her with a strong academic foundation in financial management, investment strategies, and economic principles. Throughout her career, she has worked in various capacities, ranging from personal banking and corporate finance to financial advisory and wealth management. Her extensive knowledge and hands-on experience have equipped her with a deep understanding of financial systems, investment strategies, and wealth-building principles.

A dedicated advocate for financial literacy, Lydiah has spent decades helping individuals and businesses navigate the complexities of finance. She has conducted financial empowerment seminars, worked closely with families to create sustainable financial plans, and guided professionals toward financial independence. She has also been deeply involved in teaching financial literacy within church communities and immigrant groups across the country, empowering individuals to achieve financial stability and independence. Her passion for teaching and mentoring has led her to share her insights in *Unleashing Financial Freedom*, a book designed to equip readers with practical tools and strategies to take control of their financial futures.

Beyond her professional achievements, Lydiah's faith has been the guiding light in her journey. She firmly believes that financial stewardship is not just about wealth accumulation but also about purpose, responsibility, and making a meaningful impact in the lives of others. Her strong faith has shaped her approach to finance, emphasizing ethical financial practices, generosity, and long-term stability. She attributes her success and perseverance to God's grace and believes that financial freedom is achievable for anyone willing to embrace knowledge, discipline, and faith-driven principles.

As a trusted financial professional, Lydiah Tate's insights in this book are drawn from real-world experience, time-tested financial principles, and a heart dedicated to empowering others. Readers can be assured that the knowledge shared in *Unleashing Financial Freedom* is not only credible but also practical, actionable, and designed to create lasting financial change. Through her words, she hopes to inspire individuals to take control of their financial journeys and live lives of abundance, security, and purpose.

Chapter 1
Introduction

Imagine a life where your choices are driven by your passions, not financial limitations. Financial freedom is the ability to live without the constant worry of money, where your savings, investments, and passive income supports your lifestyle, freeing you from the need to rely on a paycheck. It's about having the autonomy to decide based on what you truly want, not what you can afford.

In this chapter, we will lay the foundation for your journey toward financial independence by exploring:

- The critical role of financial education in shaping your financial future
- How financial independence differs from simply being rich, and why both are important
- The impact of poor financial habits and the steps you can take to break free from them
- A practical roadmap to achieving financial stability and long-term security

By the end of this book, you'll have a clear understanding of the core financial principles that will guide and help you take confident steps toward mastering your finances and securing your future.

What is Financial Freedom?

Financial freedom is the ability to make life choices without being burdened by financial constraints. It means having sufficient savings, investments, and passive income to sustain your lifestyle without depending on a paycheck.

How to Achieve Financial Freedom:

1. Understand your financial situation – Take stock of your income, expenses, debts, and assets.
2. Set clear financial goals – Define what financial freedom means to you and create a plan to achieve it.
3. Develop good money habits – Build strong budgeting, saving, investing, and debt management skills.
4. Create multiple streams of income – Increase financial security through diversification.
5. Build an emergency fund – Prepare for unexpected financial events.
6. Invest for the future – Grow wealth through investments in stocks, bonds, real estate, and businesses.
7. Manage Financial Risks appropriately
8. Empower your generation

This chapter sets the stage for the journey toward financial freedom. It explores the importance of financial education, common financial struggles, and the benefits of mastering money management. Readers will be introduced to the fundamental financial concepts covered in the book and how they can apply them to their lives.

The fundamental financial concepts form the core knowledge necessary for managing money, making informed financial decisions, and achieving financial stability and growth. Here are some key concepts:

1. Income

Income refers to the money you earn through your job, investments, or other sources. It's the starting point of any financial plan, and understanding how much you earn helps you allocate money effectively.

2. Budgeting

Budgeting is the process of creating a plan for how you will spend your money. It involves tracking your income and expenses, setting limits, and prioritizing needs over wants to ensure you live within your means and save for future goals.

3. Savings

Saving is the act of setting aside a portion of your income for future needs, emergencies, or long-term goals. It involves building an emergency fund, saving for big purchases, and ensuring you have a financial cushion.

4. Debt Management

Debt management involves understanding how to handle and repay loans or credit card balances. It includes managing your debt-to-income ratio, using debt responsibly, and adopting strategies like the snowball or avalanche method to pay off debt efficiently.

5. Investing

Investing is putting money into assets that have the potential to grow over time, such as stocks, bonds, real estate, or retirement accounts. Understanding risk tolerance, diversification, and compounding is key to growing your wealth through investments.

6. Credit and Credit Scores

Credit refers to the ability to borrow money or access goods and services before payment, often based on your creditworthiness. Your credit score is a numerical representation of your credit history and is crucial for securing loans, and mortgages, and getting favorable interest rates.

7. Financial Independence and Retirement

Financial independence means having enough income from savings, investments, and passive income to cover living expenses without a paycheck. Planning for retirement involves saving and investing to ensure you can maintain your lifestyle in later years without working.

8. Risk Management and Insurance

Insurance is a form of risk management that protects you against financial losses from events such as accidents, illness, or property damage. Understanding different types of insurance (health, life, auto, home) is essential for protecting yourself and your family from unexpected costs.

9. Taxation

Taxes are your contributions to government revenue, affecting your disposable income. Understanding how taxes work, including income tax, capital gains, and tax-deferred accounts like 401(k)s and IRAs, helps you manage your finances efficiently.

10. Compound Interest

Compound interest refers to the process where interest earned on an investment is added to the principal so that interest is earned on the original amount as well as the accumulated interest. This concept is crucial for understanding how investments grow over time.

11. Net Worth

Net worth is the difference between what you own (assets) and what you owe (liabilities). It indicates your financial health and helps you understand where you stand regarding wealth.

12. Financial Planning and Goal Setting

Financial planning involves setting short- and long-term financial goals, creating a roadmap to achieve them, and adjusting your plans as circumstances change. Clear goals, whether for buying a home, paying off debt, or retiring early, help guide your financial decisions.

Each of these concepts works together to provide a strong financial foundation. Mastering them allows individuals to make informed decisions, build wealth, and ultimately achieve financial freedom.

Chapter 2
Budgeting

2.1 What is Budgeting?

One simple definition of budgeting is the process of creating a financial plan that outlines income and expenses. This section explains why budgeting is essential, how it helps manage money effectively, and how it provides financial stability.

Types of Budgeting

Different budgeting methods exist, and selecting the right one depends on individual financial goals and lifestyle. This section covers:

- Zero-based budgeting
- The 50/30/20 rule
- Envelope system
- Line-item budgeting
- Reverse budgeting

Choosing a Budget Technique

A guide to identifying the best budgeting approach based on income, expenses, and financial goals. This section offers real-life scenarios to help readers choose the most suitable budgeting method.

Breakdown of Cost-of-Living Budgeting Categories

This section provides an in-depth look at the key expense categories in a budget, such as housing, transportation, food, healthcare, debt payments, and entertainment.

Easy Steps to Budgeting

A step-by-step approach to creating and sticking to a budget, from assessing income to adjusting for unexpected expenses.

Budgeting-Cash Flow Management

You have an income and you definitely have expenses, the juggling process to balance the two is budgeting. In this module, we will learn how to harness this process to strengthen our financial well-being.

Budgeting is simply balancing your expenses with your income. If they don't balance and you spend more than you make, you will have a problem. Many people are unaware that they spend more than they earn and are accumulating debt year after year.

The process of budgeting includes making a strategy for how you will spend your money. A budget is the term for this spending strategy. Having a plan allows you to know ahead of time if you will have enough money to do the things you need or want to do.

This budget usually necessitates keeping track of two things: your after-tax income and the amount you spend each month.

At the most basic level, you want your monthly expenses, including savings and debt payments to amount to less than your take-home pay. Later, you may change your spending to suit your objectives, pay off debt faster, retire well, or indulge yourself.

Why is Budgeting So Important?

Budgeting ensures that you always have enough money for the things you need and the things that are essential to you since it helps you set a spending plan for your money. Following a budget or spending plan might help you avoid debt or get out of it if you're presently in it.

Action Item

1. List down 5 areas where budgeting will improve your finances.

2.2 Types of Budget

It's best to know where you stand financially before deciding on a budgeting plan. You may do this by keeping track of all of your after-tax income and expenses.

This will give you a sense of how aware you are of your money. It will also assist you in determining budget categories, that are required for basically every budgeting strategy.

It's also a good idea to keep track of your expenses for a month. This will assist you in determining where your money is being spent. It's best to know where you stand financially before deciding on a budgeting plan. You may do this by keeping track of all of your after-tax income and expenses.

This may be accomplished by simply keeping track of everything you spend money on. It makes no difference whether you pay your expenses with cash, a credit card, or a debit card, make a note of it.

However small the amount it doesn't matter. You should track all of your spending and categorize it because you will need this information later when creating your budget.

1. Cash Envelope

This is where we use cash to pay bills, when you first start budgeting, you'll need to figure out how much money you'll need in each of your budget categories.

The specified quantities of cash would then be placed in separate envelopes labeled with the relevant budget category. You'll take cash from the proper envelope when you start paying your bills throughout the month.

People who are familiar with working with cash will benefit from this budgeting approach. It is regarded as a form of rigorous budgeting. There is no more money to spend once the money in an envelope has been spent.

If you have problems keeping to your budget or overpaying with debit cards, the cash envelope budgeting approach is ideal. It is more probable that when dealing with cash, some people spend less.

2. Zero-Based

It's a straightforward budgeting approach in which your income less your spending must equal zero.

This method of budgeting is ideal for those who have a fixed monthly income or can accurately predict their monthly income. Because all of your money must be accounted for, it is regarded as a rigorous budgeting approach.

This approach works well for experienced budgeters.

3. 50-30-20 Rule

A proportionate budgeting system or a percentage-based budget is another name for the 50-30-20 Rule budgeting approach. It's a way of budgeting in which you divide your budget into categories and allocate a percentage to each one.

Your after-tax income is divided into three categories in the 50/30/20 budget: Needs are 50% of the budget, wants are 30% of the time, and savings/debt is 20% of the time.

This budget is ideal for beginners since it does not need a precise recording of all of your spending. Because your spending in each area might fluctuate from month to month, it's termed a flexible budgeting technique. All you have to do now is stick to your established % categories. You may also tailor the percentages for each area to your requirements.

If you have a lot of debt or want to save a lot of money, the 50-30-20 Rule budget isn't ideal.

1. **Pay-Yourself-First**

The Pay-Yourself-First budget is a straightforward budgeting approach in which you set aside a fixed amount for savings and debt repayment, then spend the rest as you wish.

Determine what proportion of your after-tax income you will "pay-yourself" each month with this sort of budget. This sum is generally set aside for a savings goal or a debt payback strategy.

You may then spend the remainder of your money any way you choose without having to keep track of it.

This budgeting method is excellent for those who have trouble saving each month or who don't want to spend too much time planning out each cost. It's a straightforward budgeting technique that focuses solely on achieving savings or debt payback goals.

Action Item

1. List down an advantage and disadvantage of each type of budget according to your spending character.

2. Identify a budget type that works for you and briefly explain why you chose it.

2.3 Choosing a Budget Technique

The key is to choose a strategy that fits your personality, individual, and finally financial goals as well as your present financial circumstances. You also have to understand what your short-term and long-term financial goals are.

Consider how much work you are prepared to put into maintaining your budget, what your major financial goals are, and how you will maintain your budget before deciding on a budgeting technique.

The first step is to choose a budgeting strategy and create a budget. You'll need to personalize your budget, keep track of it each month, and stick to it.

This is why it's critical to pick the proper budgeting technique for you. You will not keep to your budget if it is too rigid or if you select a way of budget management that is too difficult for you.

Budgeting Software

After you've decided on a budgeting plan that works for you, you'll need to figure out how you'll stick to it. If you want to manage your money electronically and on the move using your smartphone, budgeting apps are the way to go.

Mint and YNAB are two popular budgeting applications. They're both compatible with iPhones and Android phones. When selecting a budgeting software, you must first decide on the budgeting technique. For example, YNAB employs the zero-based budgeting technique, which requires each dollar to be assigned a task.

Action Item

i. Choose a budgeting method that best fits your personality and income

ii. Construct a budget from the income and expenditure you came up with in module 1. Be sure to include savings in this.

iii. Download a savings App and use it to the best of your ability, ensure you have your budget both in the app and manual. (In your PC or written down) Choose a preferred software solution.

2.4 Breakdown of Cost-of-Living Budgeting Categories

"Acknowledge" Budgeting, being a fundamental component of financial growth, has attracted notable interest in research analysis. In the following breakdown, you will find a tried and tested recommendation for your budgetary allocation for an average household. As we go through the expense items and recommended allocation compare with what you currently spend and the adjustments you might have to make.

- **Food: 10 – 20%**
- **Clothing: 3 – 5%**
- **Transportation: 15 – 20%**
- **Housing: 35%**
- **Utilities: 5%**
- **Medical: 3%**
- **Debt Payments: 5 – 15%**

Many people find that their budget is quite tight because their monthly debt payments are closer to 25% of their net income. Subsequent modules will instruct on how this percentage can be achieved.

- **Savings: 5 – 10%**

Make a plan to save money for non-recurring monthly costs as well as for the future. Then you'll have some additional cash on hand when you need it.

- **Personal and recreational spending: 5–10%**

Please note how comprehensive this breakdown is; it includes almost all costs, even emergencies, which are covered by funds set aside for a rainy day.

Action Item

1. From your budget, classify all your expenses as above and note down the resulting percentages compared to your total income.

2.5 7 Easy Steps to Budgeting

Get back to basics with a budget you can stick to and avoid a potential personal financial disaster. Here's where to begin:

Steps to Budgeting.

1. Set realistic objectives.

Setting financial goals will assist you in making wise financial decisions. Consider the following question: How do you want your money to look in a year? Decide what matters most to you and begin there.

2. Determine your earnings and expenses.

You undoubtedly have a good idea of how much money you make each month, but do you know where it all goes? Find out by keeping track of your spending. Spend like you normally would, but keep track of every penny for a few weeks. It's simple, and the results will astound you.

3. Separate Needs from wants

Consider if you really want or need something. Will spending this money get me closer or further away from my financial goals? Is it possible for me to live without it? When you establish clear priorities for yourself, making decisions becomes easier.

4. Plan Your Budget

Check to see whether you're spending more than you're earning. Make sure you have enough money in your budget to cover all you need to pay for. A free, easy-to-use budget calculator spreadsheet and worksheet is one simple method to achieve this.

5. Implement Your Strategy

Make sure your spending corresponds to when you are paid. Make a plan for how you'll spend each paycheque ahead of time. Consider this: Have I budgeted for my basic needs (shelter, food, utilities, transportation, and so on)? Have I set aside money for debt payments, unforeseen needs, savings, and fun? You will be protected against more debt since you will not be relying on credit to pay for your living costs.

6. Deal with Seasonal Expenses

Things will "just come up" - school costs, new shoes, or annual membership, for example. Set money aside to cover these costs so you don't fall into debt.

7. Look ahead

It might take a month or two to get back on track with your budget. Allow yourself time to adjust if you've been living without a budget for a long period. If things aren't going as planned, don't be hesitant to seek assistance.

How to Identify the Best Budgeting Tool

Choosing the best budgeting tool for your needs can be a crucial step toward achieving your financial goals, managing your money effectively, and avoiding financial stress. With so many budgeting tools available—ranging from apps and software to spreadsheets—finding the right one depends on your personal preferences, financial goals, and the features that align with your lifestyle. Here's how to identify the best budgeting tool for you:

Step 1: Determine Your Budgeting Goals

The first step is to assess your financial goals and understand what you need from a budgeting tool. Different tools may be more suited to different purposes, so being clear on your goals will help you narrow your options.

- **Track Expenses:** If your primary goal is to track your spending and ensure you're staying within budget, you'll need a tool that provides clear, easy-to-read expense categories and alerts.
- **Save for Specific Goals:** If you want to save for a particular goal, such as buying a house, paying off debt, or building an emergency fund, look for a tool that allows you to set goals and track your progress.
- **Monitor Net Worth:** If you're more focused on long-term wealth-building and net worth tracking, find a budgeting tool that lets you see all your assets and liabilities in one place.

Step 2: Consider Your Personal Preferences

Think about your preferences when it comes to managing your finances. Do you prefer using a desktop app, a mobile app, or a simple spreadsheet? How hands-on do you want to be in the budgeting process? Your comfort with technology will influence which tool works best for you.

- **Ease of Use:** Choose a tool that's intuitive and easy for you to navigate. You don't want to waste time trying to figure out how to use the tool. Look for a user-friendly interface that matches your tech comfort level.
- **Customization:** Some people prefer highly customizable tools that allow them to create categories, set rules, and adjust features as needed. Others may want something simpler with predefined categories.
- **Accessibility:** If you want access to your budget from multiple devices, make sure the tool offers cloud-based storage, syncing across devices, or a mobile app version.

Step 3: Evaluate Features and Functionality

The best budgeting tool will offer features that meet your needs and enhance your budgeting experience. Here are some important features to consider:

- **Expense Tracking:** The ability to track and categorize your expenses automatically is a must-have. Look for tools that sync with your bank accounts, credit cards, and other financial accounts to automatically import transactions.

- **Budget Creation:** A good budgeting tool should allow you to create a personalized budget that's based on your income, expenses, and financial goals. Some tools also offer templates to get started quickly.

- **Bill Tracking & Reminders:** If you have multiple recurring bills, a budgeting tool with bill-tracking features can help you stay on top of due dates. Look for reminders or automatic payments to avoid late fees.

- **Financial Goal Setting:** The best tools will help you set specific goals (e.g., saving for a vacation, paying off debt) and track your progress over time. Some apps offer features that let you allocate money to different goals automatically.

- **Debt Tracking & Management:** If paying down debt is a priority, find a tool with debt-tracking features, such as the ability to see all your debts in one place, track payments, and prioritize high-interest debt.

- **Reporting and Insights:** A budgeting tool with reporting features can give you a deeper understanding of your financial habits. Look for charts or visualizations that help you see trends in your spending, savings, and overall progress.

Step 4: Check for Compatibility with Your Financial Accounts

Ensure that the budgeting tool you choose is compatible with the bank accounts, credit cards, and financial institutions you use. Some tools have more integration options than others.

- **Bank Syncing:** Many budgeting tools allow you to sync directly with your bank accounts and credit cards to track spending automatically. Check whether the tool supports automatic syncing with your accounts to avoid manual input.

- **Import Transactions:** For a more hands-off approach, choose a tool that allows you to import or sync transactions directly from your financial accounts. This reduces the time you spend entering data manually.

Step 5: Look for Mobile Accessibility

If you're someone who prefers to track your budget on the go, a mobile app with strong functionality is essential. Look for budgeting tools that offer apps for both iOS and Android devices, as well as web-based versions that sync across devices.

- **Cross-Device Synchronization:** Ensure the tool syncs across multiple devices so you can track and adjust your budget from anywhere, whether at home or on the go.

- **Ease of Use on Mobile:** Check that the mobile version has all the key features you need and that it's easy to use, whether you're adding a transaction, checking your progress, or setting goals.

Step 6: Consider Security Features

Your financial data is sensitive, so security should be a top priority when selecting a budgeting tool.

- **Data Encryption:** Make sure the tool uses encryption to protect your financial data. This helps ensure that your information remains private and secure.

- **Multi-Factor Authentication:** Some tools offer multi-factor authentication (MFA), which adds an extra layer of security. This feature is especially helpful for tools that sync with your bank accounts or store sensitive financial data.

- **Privacy Policy:** Review the tool's privacy policy to understand how your data is used and whether it is shared with third parties. Some tools may sell your data or use it for targeted marketing, which could be a dealbreaker for some users.

Step 7: Look at Cost and Subscription Options

The best budgeting tool is one that fits within your budget. While there are free tools available, many premium tools offer advanced features for a subscription fee.

- **Free vs. Paid Tools:** Many budgeting tools have free versions with basic features, but you may need to pay for a premium version to access advanced features like bill tracking, investment tracking, or goal-setting. Determine whether the extra cost is worth the added functionality.
- **Trial Period:** Many paid budgeting tools offer free trials, so take advantage of these to test out the tool before committing to a subscription.
- **Cost Transparency:** Ensure that you clearly understand any fees associated with the tool. Some tools charge a monthly or annual fee, while others may have a one-time cost. Be wary of hidden fees or unexpected charges.

Step 8: Read User Reviews and Ratings

To get a better sense of how a budgeting tool works in real life, read reviews and ratings from other users. These reviews can provide insights into the usability, features, and customer service of the tool.

- **App Store Reviews:** If you're considering a mobile app, check the reviews on the App Store (iOS) or Google Play (Android) to see what other users think.
- **Online Forums and Blogs:** Look for discussions on personal finance forums, blogs, or communities like Reddit. People often share their experiences and recommend budgeting tools based on their personal experiences.

- **Customer Support:** Good customer support is important, especially when you encounter issues with syncing, billing, or technical problems. Check if the tool has a helpful support team with easily accessible contact options.

Step 9: Test the Tool

Once you've narrowed down your options, test out a few tools to see which one feels the most comfortable for you. Many budgeting apps have free versions or trial periods that let you experiment without making a long-term commitment.

- **Ease of Setup:** Evaluate how easy it is to set up your account, input your financial data, and create your first budget.

- **User Interface:** Ensure the interface is intuitive and that you can easily find the features you need.

- **Help and Support:** See if the tool provides tutorials or guides to help you get started. Look for responsive customer support if you run into any issues during your trial.

Conclusion

The best budgeting tool for you depends on your unique financial situation, goals, and preferences. By understanding your goals, evaluating features, and testing different tools, you can identify the tool that best helps you take control of your finances. Consider the ease of use, cost, security, and ability to sync with your financial accounts as key factors when making your decision. Remember, the right budgeting tool will not only help you manage your money better but will also empower you to achieve your financial goals more effectively.

Chapter 3
Debt Management

3.1 What is Debt?

Debt is borrowed money that must be repaid, often with interest. It can be a tool for financial growth or a burden if mismanaged. This section explains the psychology of debt and why people fall into debt traps.

Understanding and Managing Debt

What is Debt? Debt occurs when you owe money to an individual, company, or institution. Any time you carry a balance that you need to pay off, it qualifies as debt. It can take many forms, such as credit card balances, loans, or mortgages.

Why It's Important to Manage Debt

Taking control of your debt requires a strong sense of purpose and persistence. Maintaining your motivation is key to staying on track. Consider how your life will improve once you are debt-free. What could you do with the extra money once you're no longer tied to paying off loans? If you're unsure of where to find motivation, here are several reasons why clearing your debt is beneficial.

1. Strengthen Your Financial Stability

Debt is a significant threat to your financial well-being because it consumes money that could otherwise be used to grow your savings. Instead of paying off loans, you could be saving for emergencies, retirement, or future goals like your children's education. Once you're debt-free, you'll have more financial freedom to focus on building long-term stability.

2. Enjoy Life Without Guilt

Ongoing debt payments can limit your ability to spend money on things that truly bring you joy. This cycle can lead to more borrowing, which worsens the financial strain. By eliminating debt, you free up funds to enjoy life more fully without constantly worrying about the financial consequences of your spending.

3. Alleviate Stress

Constantly thinking about how to cover debt payments can lead to high levels of stress, which may even affect your health. Chronic stress is linked to issues such as migraines, anxiety, and heart problems. Becoming debt-free can help reduce this stress and improve your well-being.

4. Simplify Your Finances

Managing debt means keeping track of multiple bills and due dates, which can be overwhelming. Once you pay off your debts, you'll only have to worry about essential monthly expenses like utilities and insurance, which don't come with interest charges or long-term commitments.

5. Boost Your Credit Score

Having high levels of debt, especially on credit cards, can hurt your credit score. When your debt balance gets too close to your credit limit, your score suffers. Paying off debts, particularly credit card balances will help raise your credit score and improve your financial health.

6. Set a Positive Example for Your Children

Children learn by example, so showing them the benefits of living debt-free can instill good money habits early on. Teach them about financial responsibility by demonstrating how living without debt can lead to more freedom and security.

7. Own What You Have

When you still owe money on assets like your home or car, you don't fully own them—the lender does. Once you pay off these secured debts, such as mortgages and car loans, you'll have true ownership of your property, eliminating the risk of foreclosure or repossession.

8. Protect Your Future Income

Every time you take on debt, you're essentially borrowing from your future earnings. Whether it's a small loan or a large mortgage, debt reduces the amount of money you'll have in the future to spend on your needs and wants. By eliminating debt now, you can maximize the value of your future income.

9. Take Control of Your Finances

When you're carrying debt, you don't have full control over your money—your lenders do. They set the terms, including how much you owe and when payments are due. In some situations, they can raise your interest rates and minimum payments, often with little warning, forcing you to quickly adjust your budget. By paying off your debt and becoming debt-free, you regain full control over your finances and can make the financial decisions that work best for you.

3.2 Types of Debt

Types of Debt: Good vs. Bad, Secured vs. Unsecured

Understanding the different types of debt is crucial to managing your finances. Debt can be categorized in several ways, each with its own set of rules, risks, and benefits. Here's a breakdown of the different types of debt to help you navigate your financial journey:

Secured Debt

Secured debt is when a loan or credit is backed by a physical asset—collateral. Common examples of secured debt include car loans, mortgages, and other types of loans tied to valuable property. When you take out a secured loan, the lender has the right to claim your asset if you fail to make the required payments. For instance, if you stop paying your mortgage or car loan, the lender can repossess the property or foreclose on your home.

The advantage of secured debt for lenders is that it provides a safety net: they either get paid back or take the collateral. However, this type of debt places more risk on the borrower. If you're unable to make your payments, you risk losing something valuable, like your car or home. Additionally, if the value of the asset depreciates (such as with cars), you could end up owing more than what the item is worth.

Unsecured Debt

Unsecured debt, on the other hand, doesn't require collateral. Common examples include credit card debt, student loans, medical bills, and personal loans. Because there's no asset backing this type of loan, lenders typically charge higher interest rates to offset the increased risk. If you fail to make payments, the lender can't seize an item from you, but they may resort to legal actions, debt collection, or lawsuits.

While unsecured debt can accumulate quickly—especially with credit cards—there's often less immediate pressure compared to secured debt. However, missing payments can lead to serious consequences, including damage to your credit score and increased financial strain.

Revolving Debt

Revolving debt refers to a type of credit where the borrower can borrow, repay, and borrow again within a set limit. The most common form of revolving debt is credit cards. With revolving debt, you have a credit limit, and as long as you make at least the minimum payment, you can continue to borrow money.

The risk with revolving debt is that the minimum payments are often very small compared to the balance you owe, meaning it's easy to fall into a cycle of borrowing more without ever paying off the full amount. Over time, this can lead to high-interest charges and significant debt accumulation. Even if you're paying off your credit card balance, the balance still technically isn't yours until it's fully paid off.

Non-Revolving Debt

Non-revolving debt refers to loans that cannot be reused once repaid. This includes loans like mortgages, auto loans, student loans, and personal loans. Unlike revolving debt, once the loan is paid off, it's closed and can't be borrowed against again.

Non-revolving debt typically involves larger loan amounts and longer repayment periods, meaning the borrower can end up paying back much more than they borrowed due to interest. While it's easier to see the tangible item you've purchased with non-revolving debt (like a home or car), it can take years to pay off and can add up significantly with interest.

Sneaky Debt

Sneaky debt includes loans or payment plans that may not seem like debt at first glance but can have hidden consequences. For example, store promotions like "zero percent APR for 90 days" or "90 days same as cash" may sound enticing, but often these offers come with high interest rates if the balance isn't paid off within the promotional period. This is a trap many fall into, as they often don't realize the steep interest rates that kick in after the promotional period ends.

Cell phone financing plans are another form of sneaky debt. When you finance a phone, you're agreeing to pay for it in installments over time. While it may seem like you're not taking on debt, the phone is essentially a secured loan, and the company can take it back if you fail to make payments. It's often better to save and buy outright with cash, rather than financing.

Good Debt vs. Bad Debt

The debate over good vs. bad debt is common, but some financial experts argue that there is no such thing as "good" debt. While some types of debt (like mortgages or student loans) may have long-term benefits, they still come with risks that can lead to financial strain if not properly managed.

Good debt is typically associated with investments that can potentially increase in value, such as a home mortgage or an education loan. These debts are seen as "good" because they contribute to long-term financial goals or growth. However, even these should be handled cautiously and repaid as soon as possible to avoid accruing excessive interest.

Bad debt, on the other hand, refers to high-interest, non-productive debt, like credit card debt or payday loans. This type of debt doesn't contribute to wealth-building and often leads to financial instability. It's important to avoid accumulating bad debt and focus on paying it off quickly to reduce interest costs.

In conclusion, while some debt can be considered an investment in your future, it's crucial to understand the different types of debt and how they can impact your finances. Whether it's securing assets or borrowing money without collateral, managing debt responsibly is key to maintaining financial health and avoiding the pitfalls of excessive borrowing.

What is Good Debt?

Good debt is typically characterized by loans or credit that are intended to improve your financial standing or come with certain tax benefits. While the concept of good debt can vary depending on personal circumstances, certain types of debt are generally considered advantageous due to their lower interest rates and potential to increase wealth or enhance your creditworthiness.

Student Loans

Although student loans are a significant burden for many graduates, they are often considered a form of good debt for two key reasons. First, student loan interest rates are generally lower than other types of debt, with federal loans offering rates between 5% and 6.6% for undergraduate and graduate students, respectively. Second, student loan interest may be tax-deductible. Borrowers can deduct up to $2,500 in interest paid on eligible loans each year, even without itemizing deductions.

Mortgages

For those who can afford it and find it beneficial for their personal situation, a mortgage is typically viewed as good debt. Mortgage loans often come with relatively low interest rates compared to other types of debt, and these rates can fluctuate daily. Additionally, many homeowners can deduct mortgage interest on loans up to $750,000 from their taxes, which can provide significant savings. This type of debt is often considered a long-term investment, as it can help you build equity in a property over time.

Home Equity Loans

Home equity loans or lines of credit allow homeowners to borrow against the value of their homes. While the tax benefits of these loans have been reduced under recent tax laws (interest on these loans is only deductible if the money is used for home improvement), home equity loans still offer relatively low interest rates, which can make them a more affordable option for borrowing. These loans are often used for home renovations, which can increase the value of the property.

Small Business Loans

When starting or growing a business, a small business loan can provide the necessary funding without giving up ownership or equity in your company. SBA-backed loans, for example, often come with competitive interest rates and favorable repayment terms. This allows entrepreneurs to maintain control over their businesses while using borrowed funds to help grow their operations. However, it's important to shop around, as online lenders and other non-traditional lenders may charge higher rates.

What is Bad Debt?

In contrast, bad debt includes high-interest loans and credit that can put your financial health at risk. These types of debt are usually associated with purchases that do not build wealth or improve your financial situation. Bad debt often leads to financial strain and can have long-term negative effects if not managed properly.

Credit Cards

Credit card debt is one of the most common types of bad debt. The average interest rate on credit cards can exceed 16%, and many cards have rates above 20%. Credit cards are a form of revolving credit, meaning that, unlike installment loans, there's no fixed repayment period. While the minimum payment may seem manageable, only making the minimum payment allows interest to accumulate, making it easy to fall into a cycle of debt that is difficult to break.

Personal Loans Used for Non-Essential Purchases

While personal loans can be used for a variety of purposes, borrowing money to finance discretionary expenses—such as vacations, luxury items, or other non-essential purchases—can be risky. The average interest rate for a personal loan is around 10.7%, but those with poor credit can face rates as high as 30% or more. Using personal loans to fund lifestyle expenses can create financial strain, especially when the repayment terms are long and interest continues to accrue.

401(k) Loans

Although taking a loan from your 401(k) can offer relatively low-interest rates, it's generally considered a poor financial decision. The main issue is that borrowing from your retirement savings means missing out on potential growth from investments. If you lose your job or switch employers while you still have an outstanding 401(k) loan, the loan becomes due within 60 days. If you're unable to repay it, the loan is treated as an early withdrawal, subject to income taxes and a 10% penalty. This can result in significant financial setbacks.

Payday Loans or Cash Advance Loans

Payday loans are extremely high-interest, short-term loans that are often marketed to individuals with poor credit. These loans can carry annual percentage rates (APRs) of 400% or more, and the repayment period is typically just two weeks. Due to their exorbitant interest rates and short repayment terms, payday loans often lead borrowers into a cycle of debt. According to the Consumer Financial Protection Bureau, a large portion of payday loans are rolled over or reborrowed within a short period, further exacerbating financial troubles and making it hard to escape the debt trap.

In summary, while some types of debt can be used strategically to enhance financial stability or fund investments, bad debt can lead to serious financial difficulties. It's important to carefully consider the terms, interest rates, and potential long-term impact of any debt before committing to it.

Easy Ways to Determine If Debt Is "Good" or "Bad"

- **Good Debt:** This type of debt is typically used for investments that have the potential to grow your wealth over time.

- **Bad Debt:** Bad debt is usually associated with borrowing money for assets that lose value over time, such as consumer goods or depreciating vehicles.
- **It Depends on Your Situation:** Not all debt falls neatly into the "good" or "bad" category. It often depends on how you manage it and your overall financial circumstances.

Can Good Debt Become Bad Debt?

How you manage debt is just as important as the type of debt itself. For example, a mortgage is usually considered good debt because it's an investment in property. However, if your mortgage payments are so high that you struggle to cover daily expenses or save for the future, it can become a financial burden, leading to what's often referred to as "house-poor" living.

Similarly, student loans are generally considered good debt as they can fund an education that improves your long-term earning potential. But if you borrow too much or don't plan carefully, the repayment burden after graduation can be overwhelming. The key is to borrow responsibly and make sure the debt doesn't hinder your ability to maintain financial stability.

Are Car Loans Good or Bad Debt?

Car loans can fall into a gray area depending on individual circumstances. If you need a car and can qualify for a low-interest rate, a car loan can be a manageable way to make a necessary purchase without draining your savings. However, if you finance an expensive car that you don't truly need or have a high-interest loan due to bad credit, it could put a strain on your finances and be considered bad debt.

Are Consolidation Loans Good or Bad Debt?

Consolidation loans can be either good or bad depending on how they are used. When used wisely, consolidation loans allow you to pay off high-interest debt, like credit card balances, more efficiently by combining everything into one loan with a potentially lower interest rate. However, if the new loan comes with higher payments or a higher interest rate, it can make your financial situation worse. It's important to make sure that consolidating debt improves your overall financial picture and doesn't create more problems.

Is Borrowing Money to Invest a Good Idea?

Some investors borrow money, known as margin borrowing, to increase their investment in stocks or other assets. This can be a strategy to amplify returns, but it's not without significant risk. Borrowing to invest only makes sense if the returns on the investment are expected to exceed the interest charges on the borrowed funds. Given the unpredictability of the market, borrowing to invest is generally not recommended for most people, as it can lead to significant losses if the market moves against you. For most people, sticking to a conservative approach and investing what you can afford without leveraging debt is a safer strategy.

Effective Methods for Paying Off Debt

When you're working to pay off your debts, it's important to have a clear strategy. Understanding the difference between good and bad debt can guide your approach. Here are some practical tips to help you pay down your debts effectively:

- **Track your debts and interest rates.** Knowing exactly where you stand with your debt and what interest rates you're paying is crucial. Ignoring your debt can only make it worse, so stay on top of it.

- **Prioritize your debt repayment.** Some financial experts suggest focusing on paying off high-interest debts first, while others recommend paying off the smallest balances to gain momentum. Choose the strategy that works best for you and your mindset.

- **Look into refinancing.** Many types of loans allow for refinancing, where you can lower your interest rate or monthly payment by adjusting your terms. If your credit has improved since you took out the loan, refinancing could be a good option.

- **Cut discretionary spending.** Freeing up more money to pay off your debts can speed up the process. Review your budget to identify areas where you can reduce spending, even if it means making temporary sacrifices.

Remember to stay focused on your goal of becoming debt-free. It may take time, but the payoff is worth the effort. Whether you're paying off a loan, saving for a major goal, or building an emergency fund, there are various strategies that can help you stay on track.

Debt Repayment Strategies

- **Debt Snowflake:** This strategy involves using small, "found" amounts of money—like spare change or unexpected windfalls—to pay down your debt. It might sound small, but every bit adds up over time.

- **Debt Snowball:** In this method, you focus on paying off your smallest debt first, regardless of the interest rate. Once that debt is cleared, you move on to the next smallest. The idea is that eliminating debt will give you a sense of accomplishment, motivating you to keep going.

- **Debt Avalanche:** This method targets the highest-interest debt first. By paying off the most expensive debts in terms of interest, you save money in the long run. Once the highest-interest balance is paid off, you move to the next highest, and so on.

Debt Management and Consolidation

- **Debt Management:** This strategy involves organizing your finances through careful planning and budgeting to bring your debt under control. By working with a debt management organization, you can develop a repayment plan with your creditors, which may help reduce the total debt or make the payments more manageable.

- **Debt Consolidation:** This option involves combining multiple debts into a single loan or payment, often at a lower interest rate. Consolidation can make your payments more affordable and expedite the process of paying off your debt.

Bankruptcy

If you're considering bankruptcy as an option, it's essential to consult with a legal professional. Bankruptcy can protect you from creditors, but it's a serious decision with long-term consequences.

After Paying Off Debt, Keep the Momentum Going

Once you've paid off a debt, it's important to keep that momentum. After paying off her last student loan, Regional Director of Wealth Nichole Baaki from Detroit didn't just stop paying the amount she'd been putting toward the loan. Instead, she directed the same monthly payment to herself by setting up an autosave rule to build her savings and invest. "Even if it's a small amount, it's better to invest that extra cash into your future rather than spend it impulsively," she says.

Use Your Credit Card Wisely

A credit card doesn't have to be viewed as extra money you don't have—it's simply a tool for managing your budget. Card Specialist Isaac Hamilton from Elgin, Illinois, sets his credit limit to match his monthly budget and uses his credit card exclusively for planned purchases. "At the end of the month, any leftover funds in my budget go directly into my savings," he says. This approach helps you manage your credit and save money at the same time.

Transfer Debt Smartly

Natina Holland, a Workforce Analytics Associate in New York City, took advantage of an offer from Chase Freedom offering 0% APR for 18 months. She transferred her balance to this card, allowing her to pay off her debt faster without accruing interest. Once the debt was cleared, she began saving for a home purchase in 2020.

Round Up Your Payments

If you're working on paying off a loan, Kimberly Harris, a CCB Technology Associate from Westerville, Ohio, suggests rounding up your monthly payments to the nearest $100—or any amount that fits your budget. Directing the extra money toward the principal helps you reduce the balance more quickly.

Automate Payments

Setting up Autopay can make paying your bills effortless and timely. Jack Mahrt, a Branch Manager from San Luis Obispo, California, shares, "Autopay ensures that I don't miss payments, so it doesn't affect my payment history if life gets busy."

Consider Taking on a Side Job

Sometimes, earning extra income can provide a significant boost in your debt payoff journey. Kari Hupfel, a Client Care Specialist in Downers Grove, Illinois, started driving for Uber as a side hustle. This extra income helped her become completely debt-free, and now she's saving for a new home.

Cut Back in Certain Areas

Gianna Graham, a KYC Officer from Tampa, Florida, was on track to pay off all her debts in 2020 until an unexpected car accident forced her to take out another loan for a new vehicle. To get back on track, she decided to cut back on travel and entertainment expenses, allowing her to focus on paying off the loan more quickly.

Managing Finances When Money is Tight

If you're experiencing a dip in income, unexpected expenses, or struggling to meet everyday costs, there are steps you can take to get back on track financially.

The first thing you need to do is determine if your income is covering all of your necessary expenses. A change in income or increased expenses often requires adjustments to your lifestyle. The sooner you evaluate your household budget; the more options you'll have to improve your situation.

Once you understand where your money is going, explore ways to make your dollars stretch further. This guide provides strategies for cutting down on everyday spending and finding extra funds to keep your finances

balanced.

It's also helpful to talk to your family and friends about your financial stress and the changes you might need to make at home. Friends can offer advice and might help you come up with creative ways to save money.

If you have children, it's important not to overwhelm them with financial worries but to let them know that your household has to adjust its spending. Involving your children in the process can teach them valuable lessons about budgeting and even contribute to the family budget, especially if they have part-time jobs. Families often become more resilient when everyone pulls together to solve financial challenges.

Your Strategic Plan for Paying Down Debt

Step 1: Create a Debt-Free Budget

The first step in your journey to becoming debt-free is understanding how much money you can reasonably put toward paying off your debt. To find this amount, track your income and expenses, using tools like your bank's online system, Mint.com, or software such as Quicken. Then, break your expenses into two categories: necessary costs (housing, groceries, utilities, transportation) and discretionary spending (entertainment, dining out, non-essential purchases). Aim to create three financial lists from the past 12 months:

- Income
- Essential Expenses
- Discretionary Expenses

Once you have this information, calculate monthly averages for each category. The next step is determining how much discretionary spending you can afford to cut back on to allocate more toward paying off your debt. While this might involve adjusting your lifestyle, it's essential to make sure the amount you decide to contribute is realistic. Setting a manageable payment amount that you can consistently meet will keep you on track, so start with a number you're comfortable with. If that amount seems too small to make a meaningful impact, consider consolidating your debt with a personal loan.

Step 2: Compile Your Debt Details

Now, make a list of all the debts you owe, such as student loans, credit card balances, store cards, and auto loans. For each debt, note down the following details:

- Lender's Name
- Total Balance
- Interest Rate
- Estimated Payoff Date

- Current Monthly Payment

You can usually exclude home mortgages from this list unless your final payment is nearing. Also, any loans with zero percent interest rates can be deprioritized.

Step 3: Choose a Debt-Repayment Strategy

With all the necessary information gathered, it's time to decide how to approach your debt repayment. Below are three popular strategies, which I like to refer to as the "wintry mix":

- **Snowflake**: This strategy involves using small, unexpected amounts of money (like spare change or the $20 bill you find in a coat pocket) to pay off your debt. While it may seem trivial, these little contributions add up.

- **Snowball**: Focus on paying off the smallest debts first, regardless of interest rates. The psychological boost of eliminating debt can help you stay motivated and disciplined in your debt repayment journey.

- **Avalanche**: My preferred method, which targets the debt with the highest interest rate first. Paying off high-interest balances first can save you money on interest charges. Once that's done, move on to the next highest rate.

You can mix and match the snowflake method with any of the other strategies for added effectiveness.

Step 4: Stick to the Golden Rule for Credit Card Use

A key rule in credit card management is to use only as much credit as you can afford to pay off in full every month. To avoid accumulating more debt while you're working toward becoming debt-free, make it a habit to follow this advice immediately.

Step 5: Consider a Personal Loan for Debt Consolidation

If you're juggling multiple high-interest debts, a personal loan could be a good option for consolidating them. These loans typically have lower interest rates than credit cards, although they can still be higher than rates on auto loans or home equity loans. A consolidation loan can lower your overall monthly payments, which may help you manage your cash flow better. However, the downside is that consolidation loans often come with longer repayment periods, which can lead to paying more interest over time.

While consolidating debt may seem like borrowing from one source to pay another, it's essential to carefully evaluate the terms and be cautious not to end up in a cycle of taking on more debt. If you opt for a personal loan, make sure it's a well-structured solution that genuinely addresses your financial situation.

Credit Card Debt: A Common and Expensive Issue

According to the U.S. Federal Reserve, approximately 80% of U.S. adults have credit cards, and more than half of them carry a balance month-to-month. On average, these "revolvers" pay over $700 annually in interest. Furthermore, a consumer survey revealed that more than half of cardholders with a balance have been carrying it for over a year.

Paying significant amounts in interest can heavily impact your finances. Additionally, carrying a balance can negatively affect your credit score, particularly if your credit utilization ratio is too high. A lower credit score can result in higher costs for other financial products, such as car loans, insurance, or cell phone plans.

For those managing multiple credit card balances, consolidating them into a single loan could simplify your finances, help you avoid missed payments, and reduce the interest charges and fees associated with multiple credit cards.

Paying Off Credit Card Debt with a Personal Loan

If you're dealing with a large balance, a personal loan might be a better option for paying off your credit card debt. Personal loans typically have lower interest rates than credit cards, which can make your payments more affordable. However, there are several factors to consider before opting for a personal loan to pay off credit card debt.

One important factor is how much debt you need to consolidate. Personal loans generally have minimum borrowing amounts between $1,000 and $5,000. Your credit score also plays a significant role in determining whether you qualify for a loan and what your interest rate will be. Some lenders may approve loans with a credit score as low as 525, while others require higher scores. Your debt-to-income ratio will also be a key consideration.

Secured loans, like home equity loans, are often easier to obtain and come with lower interest rates and higher borrowing limits. However, using your home as collateral increases your risk—you could lose your home if you default on the loan. Unsecured loans, the more common option for credit card debt consolidation, rely on your financial data and credit score for approval.

What to Expect from a Personal Loan

Personal loans, whether secured or unsecured, are typically paid off in fixed monthly installments over a set term, ranging from one to five years. A debt repayment calculator can help you estimate your monthly payments. While personal loans generally offer lower interest rates than credit cards, they might still cost you more over time if you choose a longer repayment period. Be sure to consider any additional fees, such as application or late fees, when evaluating loan options.

The advantage of a personal loan, unlike revolving credit card debt, is that it typically does not negatively impact your credit score. In fact, it could improve your credit score if you make your payments on time.

Online lending platforms offer easy comparisons and reviews of personal loans. Research suggests that personal loan interest rates are, on average, 4% lower than credit card rates. However, if your credit score is low, the difference might not be as significant.

In recent years, fintech lenders have gained a substantial share of the personal lending market. By 2019, they commanded about 30% of the market. Research by the Federal Reserve found that many consumers who used personal loans to pay off their credit card debt saved money and improved their credit scores.

Transferring Your Balance to a New Card

An alternative to using a personal loan is transferring your credit card balances to a new card, especially if your debt is relatively small. Some cards offer a 0% introductory APR for balance transfers for up to 15 months, though you may be required to pay a balance transfer fee. Be sure to read the terms carefully to confirm the offer applies to transfers and not just new purchases.

Pros and Cons of Personal Loans for Credit Card Debt

Pros:

- Lower interest rates
- Predictable monthly payments
- Potential to improve your credit score

Cons:

- Unexpected fees may apply
- Longer repayment periods could end up costing more
- Difficulty qualifying with a low credit score

Plan Before Committing to a Loan

Before taking out a personal loan or transferring your balance, it's essential to plan, budget, and economize. Ensure you know exactly how much you will pay each month and how you'll fund it. Without this planning, late fees or interest rate increases could set you back.

Think about how you accumulated debt in the first place. If unnecessary spending is contributed, financial advisors recommend cutting back on those expenses. Otherwise, you may end up in a cycle of debt.

A practical tip is to pay more than the minimum monthly payment on your debt consolidation loan to shorten its repayment term. For example, if you consolidate several loans and reduce your monthly payments by 40%, apply part of the saved money towards paying off the consolidation loan faster.

Step 6: Accelerate the Plan

Take your repayment plan to the next level by selling unused items around the house. Whether it's electronics, jewelry, or furniture, selling things you no longer need could generate hundreds of dollars each month. Consider using the proceeds to pay off your debt faster.

Debt is classified into:

- Secured Debt – Backed by collateral (e.g., mortgage, auto loans)
- Unsecured Debt – No collateral (e.g., credit cards, personal loans)
- Revolving Debt – Can be borrowed repeatedly (e.g., credit lines)
- Non-Revolving-Installment Debt – Fixed payments over time (e.g., student loans)

Understanding the differences helps in prioritizing repayment strategies.

3.3 How to Avoid Debt

Preventive measures include:

- Living within your means
- Using cash instead of credit
- Building an emergency fund
- Practicing mindful spending

3.4 Maneuvering Through Debt

If already in debt, strategies include:

- Debt consolidation
- Balance transfer credit cards
- Refinancing loans
- Negotiating lower interest rates

3.5 Debt Strategy

Effective debt repayment strategies include:

- Snowball Method – Paying off the smallest debts first
- Avalanche Method – Tackling the highest-interest debt first
- Debt Settlement – Negotiating to pay less than owed

Conclusion

Managing debt effectively is an essential step toward a secure and fulfilling financial future. By paying off your debts, you can unlock more freedom, enjoy better financial health, and make room for long-term wealth-building. Take control of your debt today, and watch as it positively transforms your financial future.

Chapter 4
Managing Credit

4.1 Understanding Credit – What is FICO and Why is It Important?

The FICO score ranges from 300 to 850 and determines creditworthiness. Factors affecting it include:

- Payment history (35%)
- Credit utilization (30%)
- Credit history length (15%)
- New credit (10%)
- Credit mix (10%)

4.2 Optimizing Credit – Debt and Credit Go Hand in Hand

This section explores:

- How to use credit wisely
- The importance of credit utilization ratios
- How responsible credit management impacts future financial opportunities

4.3 Managing Negative Reports

How to dispute credit report errors, rebuild credit after a financial setback, and improve credit scores over time.

Even if you've never owned a credit card, activities such as taking out loans or paying utility bills can contribute to your credit history. The three primary credit reporting agencies—Experian, TransUnion, and Equifax—assess your creditworthiness based on this information.

A credit score is a three-digit number that encapsulates your credit history. It predicts the likelihood of you falling 90 days or more behind on credit card or loan payments within the next two years, which is why lenders often refer to them as risk scores.

There are two predominant credit scoring models: FICO and VantageScore, among others. Due to differences in calculation and reporting methods, you might have multiple credit scores. Understanding these scoring models can empower you to make informed decisions to foster a positive financial future.

Achieving a FICO score of 800 is a commendable goal. Individuals within this "Excellent" range are more likely to receive credit approvals and benefit from favorable terms and interest rates. Lenders have high confidence in borrowers with such scores, as they are deemed low-risk. According to Experian, only 21% of Americans possess excellent scores, with fewer than 1% anticipated to become seriously delinquent in the future.

For instance, with a FICO score of 760 or higher, you might qualify for a 60-month auto loan at an interest rate as low as 3%. An 800 FICO score could also present opportunities to refinance existing loans under more favorable terms, potentially reducing your monthly payments.

Maintaining a good credit score offers numerous advantages, such as easier approval for loans and credit cards, lower interest rates, higher credit limits, and faster approval processes. Additionally, a strong credit score can result in better rental opportunities, fewer utility deposits, the ability to qualify for premium credit card rewards, improved insurance rates, and even job prospects, as some employers consider credit history during hiring. It's crucial to maintain a good credit score by paying bills on time, keeping credit utilization low, and avoiding unnecessary credit applications. A good credit score signals responsible financial management and can significantly impact multiple aspects of personal and financial life. investopedia.com

In summary, understanding and managing your credit score is vital for securing favorable financial opportunities and ensuring long-term financial health.

Understanding Credit: The Significance of FICO Scores and Their Benefits

In our digitally interconnected world, numerous websites and applications monitor user activities. Similarly, credit reporting agencies track your financial payment history. These agencies compile detailed, objective reports of your financial behavior, which are then used to calculate your credit score—a numerical representation of your financial reliability.

Even if you've never owned a credit card, activities like taking out loans or paying utility bills can lead to the major credit reporting agencies—Experian, TransUnion, and Equifax—assessing your creditworthiness.

A credit score is a number that summarizes your credit history. There are two dominant credit scoring models—FICO and VantageScore—and many other lesser-used models. Because of variations in how scores are calculated and reported, you may have multiple credit scores. Understanding how scores are calculated can help you take action to establish a positive financial future.

A credit score is a three-digit number that summarizes your credit history. It predicts for lenders the likelihood you might fall 90 days or more behind in your credit card or loan payments during the next two years. That's why lenders sometimes call them risk scores.

What Constitutes an Excellent Credit Score?

Achieving a FICO score of 800 is the ultimate goal for many—and there's good reason for that: People in the Excellent credit score range are the most likely to be approved for a credit card or loan, and they're also likely to get the best available terms and/or interest rates. That's because lenders have a high degree of confidence that people with scores in this range will repay their debts. Only 21% of Americans have excellent scores, and fewer than 1% of them are likely to become seriously delinquent in the future, according to Experian.

Advantages of a High Credit Score

Better terms. For example, if your FICO score is 760 or better, you could qualify for a 60-month auto loan at an interest rate as low as 3%, experts say. Achieving an 800 FICO score may also open opportunities to reduce your monthly payments by refinancing older loans on better terms.

The Concept of a "Perfect" Score

Experts consider any FICO score of 800 or above as "perfect," meaning that striving for an even higher score probably won't get you better terms. It's also noteworthy that the VantageScore range is slightly different: any score of 781 or higher is seen as Excellent—likely due to the broader scoring range used by VantageScore.

The Elusive 900 Score

You may have heard rumors of credit scores as high as 900—or even higher. In reality, a 900 score is either impossible or only relevant in special cases, experts say. Unlike the unicorns, a 900 score does exist. But it occurs only in earlier versions of the VantageScore scale that are no longer used, and in the FICO Auto Score used for car loans.

Implications of the Very Good/Good Range

If your credit score falls into the next-to-highest range, experts say the odds of approval for loans or credit are good—and if you are approved you'll likely be offered better-than-average interest or terms.

The Middle: Good/Fair

You can generally still borrow money if you fall into the middle credit score ranges, but it may be more challenging. Experts say that it begins to be less likely that you'll be approved for loans and you may be offered less-competitive terms. The average interest rate on 60-month auto loans is 5.27%, and people with scores in the good/fair range—which is slightly below average—should expect to pay slightly higher rates, according to one analysis.

Defining a Poor Credit Score

Experts note that applicants in these ranges are generally seen as subprime borrowers. That means they are less likely to be approved for loans, and will likely be offered higher-than-average interest rates and/or be asked to make a deposit. For example, someone with a 580 FICO score might expect to pay an interest rate 5 or 10 times higher than someone with an average or better score. Applicants for mortgages insured by the Federal Housing Administration (FHA) who have scored lower than 580 may still qualify, but only if they meet other requirements and make a 10% deposit as opposed to a minimum of 3.5% for higher-scoring applications.

At the Lowest End of the Credit Score Spectrum

If your score falls in the bottom "Very Poor" credit score range, experts say it's unlikely you will be approved for mainstream credit. To borrow, you will likely have to make a deposit in exchange for a secured line of credit. Other options may be costly "small-dollar" loans (such as auto title or payday loans) with interest rates that experts say average 391%.

Assessing Your Credit Score Range

As you evaluate the implications of your credit score, keep in mind that lenders typically also consider other factors, which could help you or hurt you. Also, experts note that lenders sometimes use their own ranges—one lender's "good" may be another's "very good." And, of course, credit scores are not frozen in time—you can take steps to improve your score.

4.2 Optimizing Credit: The Interplay Between Debt and Credit

How, Where, When, and Why to Check Your Credit Score

From completing a credit application to securing the most competitive mortgage rates, your credit score is an important number that tells lenders your level of creditworthiness. That's why it's helpful to regularly keep tabs on your score, especially since your score is calculated each month and may be affected by opening a new credit line or paying down debt.

Checking your own credit score is known as a "soft check," which won't affect your score and will not appear on your credit report.

Regularly monitoring your credit score—ideally on a monthly basis—enables you to track your financial progress, identify and correct errors that may be negatively impacting your score, and establish informed financial goals for the future.

Where to Access a Free Credit Score

Numerous online platforms provide free access to your credit score, including services offered by banks and credit card issuers. While some companies may charge for credit score access, often bundling it with personalized financial advice, there are comprehensive free services available as well.

For instance, American Express's MyCredit Guide offers complimentary credit score checks, monthly credit report views, and a credit score simulator to help you understand how actions like paying down debt, closing accounts, or applying for new credit can influence your score.

Why Regular Credit Score Monitoring Matters

Your credit score plays a crucial role in loan approvals, lease agreements, and securing favorable interest rates and credit card offers. Here are five reasons to make regular credit score monitoring a habit:

1. **Assess Your Financial Standing**

Credit scores range from poor to excellent. Individuals with "very good" or "excellent" scores typically enjoy lower interest rates on loans and credit lines, along with premium rewards. Knowing your score helps you maintain and develop healthy credit habits.

2. **Develop a Strategy to Improve Your Score**

If your score falls within the "fair" or "good" categories, proactive steps can boost it. Factors influencing your score include credit history length, payment punctuality, types of loans, and credit utilization ratio (the amount of debt relative to available credit). While some elements, like payment history, may be challenging to amend, increasing credit limits or paying down debt can lower your credit utilization ratio, potentially raising your score. Tools like MyCredit Guide analyze your current credit status to provide actionable insights for improvement.

3. **Maintain Financial Health**

Minor fluctuations in your credit score are normal—for example, a slight dip after applying for a new credit card or loan. However, a persistent decline signals the need for intervention. Regularly checking your score alerts you to issues requiring attention before they escalate.

4. **Prepare for Credit or Loan Applications**

Lenders and credit card issuers use your credit score to quickly assess your likelihood of repaying debt. Being aware of your score allows you to identify loans and credit cards that align with your credit profile. Many financial products specify minimum credit score requirements, so knowing your score can prevent unsuccessful applications.

5. **Access Your Credit Report**

In addition to monitoring your credit score, reviewing your credit report is advisable. MyCredit Guide provides access to your TransUnion credit report, enabling you to verify accuracy and understand how actions like late payments or debt settlements affect your score. Reporting errors to credit bureaus can lead to immediate score improvements.

By staying informed about your credit score and report, you can make strategic decisions to enhance your financial well-being.

Which Type of Credit Score Should You Check?

There are two primary credit score models: VantageScore and FICO. Both have slightly different scoring ranges and may calculate scores differently, with each placing varying emphasis on factors like credit history or credit utilization ratio. While the specific score may differ between models, your credit score is likely to be classified in a similar range for both VantageScore and FICO.

It's important to understand the scoring ranges for each model and know which credit score you're receiving when you sign up for a free credit score online. For example, MyCredit Guide uses VantageScore® 3.0 Credit Score from TransUnion. If you're applying for a specific type of loan, it's helpful to know which scoring model the lender uses prior to application to see if your score falls into an appropriate range.

While your credit score may differ between models, positive credit behaviors such as paying bills on time and keeping your credit utilization ratio low will help maintain good scores across both models.

How Can I Improve My Credit Score?

The only way to know with certainty how a specific action or financial decision will affect your credit score is to implement it. However, using a credit score simulator can provide a good estimate of the likely impact of various financial changes.

Credit score simulators allow you to explore how actions like improving your on-time payment history, closing an account, or requesting a higher credit limit might affect your score. Since these tools rely on unique data from your own credit profile, they can help you understand potential changes before taking action.

Explore Free Credit Score Simulators

To evaluate these tools, I tried out three credit score simulators:

- Credit Karma Simulator
- NerdWallet Simulator
- American Express' MyCredit Guide Simulator

All three are free and easy to use, making them a natural starting point. However, keep in mind that more simulators are available. Many banks and financial service providers now offer these tools, though some charge fees, typically as part of a broader service package that might include free credit reports, monitoring, and fraud protection.

How Credit Score Simulators Reveal the Impact of Your Actions

Each simulator I used had preset actions and allowed me to customize simulations by filling in details and using drop-down lists. The great thing is that running simulations won't impact your actual credit score, so it's an opportunity to experiment with different scenarios and compare their effects.

I tested out a few potential actions, like increasing my credit limit by $1,000, and also experimented with more extreme situations, such as letting an account go into collections. The results were eye-opening, with some actions having much greater effects than others.

For example, increasing my credit limit by $1,000 didn't impact my score at all. But if I upped it by $2,500, my score would increase by just one point. On the other hand, opening a new credit card with a $1,000 limit was estimated to lower my score by six points. These comparisons were valuable because they gave me insight into which actions were best for my credit score.

Other findings were equally surprising. Allowing one account to become 30 days past due didn't change my score, but letting all accounts fall 30 days behind would result in an estimated 122-point drop. If just one account went into collections, my score would drop by about 45 points. Paying off the balance on one card would only increase my score by one point while clearing all balances resulted in a 47-point boost.

In conclusion, using these simulators helped me clearly understand how different financial actions could impact my credit score, often with surprising results.

How Often Does Your Credit Score Update?

If you're working on improving your credit, you might wonder how frequently your credit score changes, especially when preparing for major purchases like a new car or applying for a mortgage. Understanding when your score updates is crucial.

There's no quick way to boost your score by 100 points overnight. Achieving an excellent credit score takes time. However, with a consistent, responsible approach to managing credit over the long run, you can expect positive results. Identify areas where you can improve, create a plan, and stick to it.

How to Boost Your Credit Score

In a nutshell: improve your score strategically. Here's how you can break it down into actionable steps:

1. Educate yourself on what factors influence your credit score.
2. Assess your individual credit situation in light of this information.
3. Pinpoint the actions that will have the most positive impact.
4. Follow a well-thought-out strategy to meet your credit score goals.

Experts emphasize the importance of being realistic. As Fair Isaac Corp. (creator of the widely-used FICO score) puts it, "Increasing your credit score is much like losing weight." In other words, lasting improvement doesn't happen instantly, and there's no one-size-fits-all solution. Many people want quick fixes, like improving their score in 30 days or increasing it by 100 or 200 points. But as Fair Isaac suggests, the best course of action is to manage your credit responsibly over time.

While your actions will determine your credit score, there are still effective ways to make a significant difference. If your score needs a boost of 200 points, there's likely room to modify your financial habits to demonstrate increased responsibility.

How Long Does It Take for Your Score to Update?

Although the process can vary, there are some general guidelines about when your credit score is updated. According to the credit bureaus, it usually takes 30 to 45 days for your activity to be reflected in your credit score. For example, TransUnion mentions that it can take a month or more for your account balance payoff to appear on your credit report. Experian recommends paying off the full balance and allowing an entire billing cycle to pass before it updates.

Sometimes, however, updates can be quicker. Credit card companies and lenders often report at the time they issue your monthly billing statements. So, if you make a payment just before the statement date, it could be reported quickly, but payments made after the statement date might take longer. Additionally, some creditors report more frequently, especially when significant changes, like paying off an account or closing it, occur.

Since each lender follows a different reporting schedule, the credit bureaus may receive updates at different times throughout the month. This means your credit score could change frequently, sometimes multiple times in a single day.

Strategic Steps to Increase Your Credit Score

Experts suggest starting your strategy by obtaining your credit reports from the three major bureaus. Without these reports, it's difficult to pinpoint the problems that need fixing or areas where improvement is possible.

You'll likely see a more noticeable score increase (like 100 points) faster if you start with a lower score. This is because there's more room for improvement, and small changes can have a bigger impact. However, be patient—improving your score is a long-term effort. Keep in mind that some strategies will definitely help boost your score.

Steps to Start Improving Your Credit Score

1. **Fix Errors on Your Credit Report:** If you spot any inaccuracies on your credit report, be sure to dispute them with the credit bureaus. Correcting these errors can help improve your score. Studies show that 21% of individuals who reviewed their credit reports discovered errors that led to updates in their credit files.

2. **Reduce Your Balances:** Experts highlight that reducing your credit utilization rate – the percentage of your available credit that you use – is one of the fastest ways to boost your score. Credit utilization makes up 30% of your FICO score, making it a major factor. It's also the most important component in the VantageScore model. Since creditors report your activity at least once a month, you don't have to wait long to see improvements. To maximize the benefit, consider

making micropayments—paying off part of your balance multiple times a month—to keep your balance lower when it's reported. Aim to keep your credit utilization under 30%, though lower is even better. I tested this using the MyCredit Guide simulator from American Express, and reducing my balances to under 30% improved my score by about 1%. Paying off my balances entirely resulted in an 8% improvement.

3. **Address Collection Accounts:** Since payment history accounts for 35% of your FICO score, any late payment, especially those 30 days or more overdue, can significantly harm your credit. Collection accounts have an even greater negative impact. If possible, negotiate a "pay for delete" agreement, where a creditor agrees to remove a collection account from your credit report in exchange for full payment. While not all collectors will agree to this, it's worth trying. Paying off a collection account won't benefit your credit score if it remains listed on your report.

4. **Get a Secured Credit Card:** If your score is low, opening a secured credit card can help boost it. To get a secured card, you deposit money into a bank account, and the bank issues a credit card with a limit equal to your deposit. If you fail to make payments, the bank keeps your deposit. To improve your score, use the card responsibly by charging small amounts and paying the balance in full and on time. Alternatively, being added as an authorized user on someone else's credit card (especially if they have a strong payment history) can also give your score a lift.

Long-Term Strategies for Improving Your Credit Score

By following the immediate actions we discussed earlier, experts suggest you start to see a slight improvement in your credit score within one to two months. However, for more substantial and lasting changes, the process takes longer and requires a consistent, strategic approach.

Here are some long-term strategies to continue improving your credit score:

1. **Pay your bills on time** consistently.

2. **Limit credit inquiries** and avoid applying for too many new credit accounts. Each inquiry can slightly lower your score.
3. **Maintain a balanced credit mix.** Having both revolving credit (like credit cards) and installment loans (like personal loans or car payments) is ideal.
4. **Build your credit history.** Keeping accounts open, even if you don't actively use them, can positively impact your credit score. Closing accounts in good standing might hurt your score.

In terms of how long it takes for positive actions, like paying down balances, to show on your credit report and improve your score, the timeline can vary. Typically, it can take a month for changes to appear on your credit report and start influencing your score. However, depending on the reporting schedules of your creditors, it could happen sooner. Similarly, negative events, like a missed payment or a high credit card balance, can also impact your score quickly.

While these timelines offer a general guideline, it's important to remember that your credit score can fluctuate multiple times within a day as information from different accounts is updated by the credit bureaus.

Credit Score Ranges

The two most commonly used credit scoring models, **FICO** and **VantageScore**, both rank credit scores on a scale from **300 to 850**. Although both models share the same range, they categorize scores into slightly different ranges, each with its own labels. Below is a chart that outlines the credit score ranges for both models:

Score Range	FICO Score	VantageScore
Excellent	750 - 850	781 - 850

Score Range	FICO Score	VantageScore
Good	700 - 749	701 - 780
Fair	650 - 699	661 - 700
Poor	600 - 649	601 - 660
Very Poor	300 - 599	300 - 600

Understanding these ranges can help you gauge where you stand and what steps you need to take to move toward a higher score.

Understanding Credit Score Ranges and Labels

Fair Isaac Corp., the creator of the FICO score, provides a breakdown of its credit score ranges and labels on its official website. According to FICO, the typical American's credit score falls within the "Good" range. However, VantageScore Solutions takes a different approach to categorizing scores. Instead of using specific labels, it divides credit scores into "credit tiers" based on the Consumer Financial Protection Bureau's (CFPB's) definition of an "average" score, which the CFPB refers to as "prime." Jeff Richardson, Vice President of Marketing & Communications at VantageScore Solutions, notes that lenders and credit bureaus ultimately determine what they consider to be a "good" credit score, as that definition can vary from one institution to another.

Here are the official VantageScore 3.0 credit tiers:

- **Superprime:** 781 - 850
- **Prime:** 661 - 780
- **Near Prime:** 601 - 660
- **Subprime:** 300 - 600

As of October 2019, the average VantageScore 3.0 was 686, which is slightly lower than the average FICO score. This discrepancy is due to VantageScore's inclusion of a broader range of consumers, many of whom tend to have lower scores.

Equifax Credit Score Ranges

In addition to FICO and VantageScore, credit scoring models vary among the major credit bureaus, with each having its own proprietary scoring method. For example, Equifax uses the following credit score ranges:

- **Excellent:** 760 - 850
- **Very Good:** 725 - 759
- **Good:** 660 - 724
- **Fair:** 560 - 659
- **Poor:** 280 - 559

It's important to note that each credit bureau may report a different score due to variations in their data and scoring algorithms.

Managing Negative Items on Your Credit Report

Your credit report plays a critical role in your financial life, influencing decisions about loans, credit cards, and even job opportunities. However, up to 21% of credit reports may contain errors significant enough to affect credit scores.

If you notice any inaccuracies in your credit report, you have the legal right to dispute them. U.S. law allows consumers to review and challenge discrepancies with the three main credit bureaus—Experian, Equifax, and TransUnion—as well as with any business that provides them information.

Common issues that could negatively impact your credit report include:

- **Errors in reporting**: These can range from incorrect personal information to outdated accounts still showing up as active.
- **Collections**: Accounts that have been sent to collections can drag down your score significantly.
- **Late payments**: Payments that are 30 days or more overdue can negatively affect your score.
- **High credit utilization**: Using over 40% of your available credit can impact your credit score.
- **Opening too many new accounts**: Each new credit inquiry can slightly lower your score.

Managing these issues effectively—such as disputing errors and paying off collections—can improve your credit score over time.

Your credit report plays a significant role in many aspects of your financial and personal life. It can influence whether you're approved for a car loan, credit card, mortgage, or even a rental apartment. Additionally, it can help uncover potential identity theft attempts. This makes it crucial to regularly review your credit reports from the three major credit bureaus—Equifax, Experian, and TransUnion—and dispute any information that is outdated, incorrect, or incomplete.

How to Dispute Your Credit Report

Disputing errors on your credit report is relatively straightforward, thanks to consumer protection laws that make the process accessible. Below are the general steps to take when disputing inaccuracies:

1. **Obtain a Copy of Your Credit Report**: Review your credit reports from all three major bureaus (Equifax, Experian, TransUnion) for any errors.

2. **Identify Errors and Write a Dispute Letter**: Write a formal dispute letter for each error you find, or fill out an online dispute form.
3. **Gather Supporting Documents**: Collect any documents that support your claim, such as bank statements, letters from lenders, or utility bills.
4. **Submit Your Dispute**: Submit your dispute online, via telephone, or by mail (certified/return receipt) according to the instructions provided by each credit bureau.
5. **Wait for Results**: Allow up to 30 days for the credit bureau to complete the dispute investigation and respond with the results.

Each of the credit bureaus has its own set of guidelines and tools for handling disputes. These include detailed instructions on the following:

- The necessary information to include in your dispute letter
- Which supporting documents are required
- How to submit your dispute
- How to track the progress of your dispute

For quicker resolution, it is recommended to file your dispute online. You can access your free credit report once a year at annualcreditreport.com, a site authorized by law and managed by the three credit bureaus. If you find errors, mark them on your report and include a copy with your dispute package.

Supporting Documents for Disputes

Each credit bureau, including Equifax, provides a list of documents that may help strengthen your dispute. These documents can include:

- Driver's license

- Birth certificate
- Utility bills
- Bank statements
- Letters from lenders
- Proof of identity theft (if applicable)
- Cancelled checks
- Bankruptcy court documents

By following the steps and providing the necessary documentation, you can effectively dispute errors on your credit report and potentially improve your credit score.

The Federal Trade Commission (FTC) has conducted several studies on credit report accuracy and dispute processes. 012, the FTC released a comprehensive study revealing that 26% of participants identified errors on their credit reports, with 21% of these disputes leading to corrections. Noy, 13% of consumers experienced a change in their credit score due to these disputes, and 5% saw their credit score improve enough to qualify for better loan terms. (ftc.gov)

In 2015, the FTC issued a follow-up study on credit report accuracy, building upon the 2012 findings.his study continued to emphasize the importance of consumers regularly reviewing their credit reports to identify dispute inaccuracies. (ftc.gov)

While these studies provide valuable insights, there have been no recent FTC studies on credit disputes beyond 2015. However, other organizations such as the Consumer Financial Protection Bureau (CFPB), have conducted more recent research on credit report disputes. For instance, a 2021 CFPB report examined the dispute process and highlighted the challenges consumers face in resolving inaccuracies. (consumerfinance.gov)

Given the evolving nature of credit reporting and dispute processes, it's advisable for consumers to stay informed through the latest resources provided by the FTC, CFPB, and other reputable organizations.

- investopedia.com
- investopedia.com

To file a credit report dispute, you'll need to gather materials that include your dispute letter, which outlines the issues and requests corrections or deletions. Various online templates are available to help craft this letter. Along with the letter, you should include any supporting documents that back up your claim. Together, these form your dispute package.

You can submit your dispute to one or more of the credit bureaus depending on where you find discrepancies. For example, Experian offers an Online Dispute Center with tools that allow you to file disputes from both computers and mobile devices. If you choose to file by mail, it's recommended to use certified mail with a return receipt to ensure your dispute is delivered. It's also important to keep records of all communications, including dates, for future reference.

What Happens After You File a Dispute?

After your dispute is filed, the credit reporting agencies must notify the information provider (such as your bank or credit card issuer) about the dispute. The provider is then obligated to verify the accuracy of the disputed information. If the data is found to be incorrect, the provider must inform the credit bureaus so they can update or remove the information. Each bureau provides a way for you to track the progress of your dispute, including possible outcomes and next steps.

Once the investigation is completed, the credit bureau must send you the results in writing, along with a new free credit report if any changes were made. Additionally, they must provide information about the data furnisher—the entity that supplied the disputed information. If desired, you can request that the bureau notify anyone who has received your credit report in the past six months about the dispute resolution.

If you're not satisfied with the outcome, you have several options:

- Refile the dispute, possibly with additional supporting documents.
- Add a statement of dispute to your file, which will be attached to any future reports. This statement can also be shared with anyone who previously accessed your credit report, though there may be a fee.

Disputing a Hard Inquiry

In addition to common errors like outdated balances or accounts that don't belong to you, credit reports may also include "hard inquiries" — requests made by third parties to review your credit report. If there are any hard inquiries that you don't recognize, these could be mistakes or signs of potential identity theft. Experts advise disputing any unrecognized hard inquiries, as too many inquiries can negatively impact your credit score.

Will Disputing Hurt Your Credit?

According to TransUnion, starting a dispute will not directly affect your credit score. However, if your dispute results in changes or removals of items on your credit report, your score could be impacted — either positively or negatively, depending on the outcome.

Your Legal Rights Under the Fair Credit Reporting Act (FCRA)

The Fair Credit Reporting Act (FCRA) grants several rights when it comes to disputing credit reports:

- You are entitled to one free credit report annually from each of the three major credit bureaus (Experian, TransUnion, and Equifax).

- You can find out who has accessed your credit report in the past year (or two years for employment-related inquiries).
- You have the right to dispute any inaccuracies directly with the credit bureau and the company that provided the information.
- If your credit application is denied based on your credit report, you are entitled to another free credit report within 60 days of the denial.
- If your dispute is unresolved, you can add a note to your report explaining the situation.

Your FICO score determines your creditworthiness. Factors include:

- 35% Payment History – Consistently making on-time payments.
- 30% Credit Utilization – Using less than 30% of your available credit.
- 15% Length of Credit History – Keeping older accounts open.
- 10% Credit Mix – Having a mix of installment and revolving credit.
- 10% New Credit – Limiting new credit applications.

4.2 Optimizing Credit – Debt and Credit Go Hand in Hand

- Pay bills on time.
- Keep credit utilization below 30%.
- Avoid unnecessary credit inquiries.

4.3 Managing Negative Reports

- Dispute credit report errors.
- Request goodwill adjustments for late payments.
- Work with credit repair agencies if necessary.

Which Credit Bureau and Credit Agency is Used by Most Lenders?

The three major credit bureaus that most lenders rely on to assess your creditworthiness are:

1. Equifax
2. Experian
3. TransUnion

Each of these bureaus collects information from lenders, credit card companies, and other financial institutions to create a credit report. Lenders use these reports to assess the risk of lending you money and determine your credit score.

Do Larger Banks Use Different Bureaus/Agencies than Smaller Banks and Credit Unions?

Lenders, including large banks, smaller banks, and credit unions, may use different credit bureaus depending on their internal policies, the type of loan, and the geographic location. While the three major credit bureaus are the primary sources, each lender may have a preferred bureau, and they might pull reports from one, two, or all three bureaus.

Large Banks: Major banks like Chase, Bank of America, and Wells Fargo may use all three bureaus (Equifax, Experian, TransUnion) when considering applications for mortgages, auto loans, or credit cards. They may also use more sophisticated scoring models that combine data from all three credit bureaus.

Smaller Banks & Credit Unions: Smaller banks and credit unions might have a preference for one or two bureaus, but they typically use the same major bureaus. However, some smaller institutions may focus more on local credit scores and might not pull all three bureaus' data.

Ultimately, each lender can select a credit bureau based on their underwriting process, the type of loan, and other factors.

Which is the Most Reliable Credit Bureau and Reporting Agency?

Each of the three major credit bureaus—Equifax, Experian, and TransUnion—has a similar mission: to collect and report information on your credit history. However, due to slight differences in the way they collect and process data, the reports they generate may differ slightly.

Equifax: Known for providing a wide range of credit monitoring services, Equifax is often seen as a reliable source for credit reporting and analytics.

Experian: Considered one of the most reliable bureaus for providing detailed credit reports and scores, Experian is also known for its fraud protection services.

TransUnion: Another well-regarded credit bureau, TransUnion tends to focus on providing comprehensive data for both consumers and businesses.

All three bureaus are reliable in terms of providing information, but the most accurate bureau for you will depend on how each reports your data, how frequently they update it, and what financial activity is reported to them.

Contact Information for the Credit Bureaus and Agencies:

Equifax

Website: https://www.equifax.com

Phone: 1-888-298-0045 (Customer service for credit report disputes)

Address:

Equifax

P.O. Box 105788

Atlanta, GA 30348

Experian

Website: https://www.experian.com

Phone: 1-888-397-3742 (Customer service for credit report disputes)

Address:

Experian

P.O. Box 9701

Allen, TX 75013

TransUnion

Website: https://www.transunion.com

Phone: 1-800-916-8800 (Customer service for credit report disputes)

Address:

TransUnion

P.O. Box 2000

Chester, PA 19016

Conclusion

The three major credit bureaus—Equifax, Experian, and TransUnion—are used by most lenders to determine creditworthiness. While larger and smaller financial institutions might have preferences for one bureau or another, they typically rely on these three bureaus. No single bureau is inherently more reliable than the others, but slight differences in data processing may affect the credit report you receive. Always monitor your credit with each bureau to ensure accuracy. Contact information for each bureau is provided for your convenience if you need to dispute any errors or obtain your credit report.

Chapter 5
Savings

What is Savings and Why is it Important?

Savings refers to the portion of income that is not spent on immediate expenses. It is crucial because life is unpredictable, and emergencies can arise at any time. Whether it's a car breaking down, a home appliance malfunctioning, or unexpected medical bills, having savings can prevent these situations from becoming overwhelming financial burdens. In this way, savings play a key role in helping individuals and families achieve financial stability and security.

Additionally, savings are essential for making larger purchases that cannot be easily covered by monthly income. For example, saving over time can help you buy an expensive item like a new car, or a camera, or fund a vacation.

How Much Money Should Be Saved?

To ensure financial security, it is generally advised that individuals or households save enough to cover at least six months of living expenses. For instance, if a household's monthly expenses total $2,000, the goal should be to save at least $12,000 ($2,000 x 6 months). To reach this goal, it's recommended that 10-20% of your net income (the amount left after taxes and deductions) be saved regularly until this target is met.

Where Can Money Be Saved?

While some people might save money in informal places like jars or piggy banks, this method is not ideal for long-term savings. Keeping money at home exposes it to risks such as theft, fire, or other disasters. A safer option is to store your money in a depository institution, which offers financial services such as savings and checking accounts. These institutions provide added protection for your money and offer opportunities to earn interest, which helps your savings grow over time.

The concept of the **time value of money** explains why money saved today is worth more than the same amount saved in the future. Depository institutions allow you to earn interest on your savings, meaning you'll receive additional funds based on a percentage of your deposited balance. This percentage is known as the **interest rate**.

Common accounts at depository institutions that earn interest include:

- **Savings accounts**: These accounts store money that is not immediately needed and can be accessed when required.
- **Money market deposit accounts**: These accounts typically offer a higher interest rate than regular savings accounts.
- **Certificates of Deposit (CDs)**: These accounts offer fixed interest rates for a specified period, typically yielding higher returns for longer commitments.

By using these options, your savings not only remain secure but also grow through interest.

Money market deposit accounts typically require a higher initial deposit to open and have restrictions on how often you can withdraw funds each month. These accounts offer a higher interest rate compared to regular savings accounts but come with some limitations on access to your money.

A **Certificate of Deposit (CD)** is another type of account that offers interest on a lump sum deposit. However, once the money is placed into a CD, it must remain there for a fixed term. If you withdraw the money before the term ends, you will incur a penalty fee. After the term concludes, you can withdraw both your principal and the interest earned. Typically, the interest rate for a CD is higher than that of a money market deposit account, and the longer you agree to leave your money in the account, the higher the interest rate tends to be. Additionally, the more money you deposit into the CD, the better the interest rate you may receive.

When saving money in these accounts, the money essentially grows on its own due to interest. The higher the interest rate, the more your savings will increase. The total amount of interest earned is also affected by how much money is saved and how long it is left in the account. For example, saving $500 at an interest rate of 3% for five years will grow to $579.64. The larger the deposit and the longer it is left in the account, the greater the return.

How to Start Saving Money

To make saving money a habit, it's important to view savings not as what's left over after spending, but as a priority. One effective strategy is called **"pay yourself first."** This means setting aside a portion of your income (typically 10-20% of your net income) for savings before using the rest for spending. By doing this, you make saving a non-negotiable part of your financial routine.

Setting personal goals is key to successfully practicing the pay-yourself-first strategy. A goal is a specific target you aim to achieve, whether it's a financial objective like saving for an emergency fund or a major purchase. By setting clear financial goals, you can direct your focus toward what matters most to you and make decisions that align with those priorities.

While setting goals, it's also important to recognize the trade-offs involved. A **trade-off** is the act of giving up one thing in exchange for another. In the case of saving money, the trade-off often involves forgoing some immediate spending in exchange for greater financial security in the future. Being aware of these trade-offs makes your savings goals more realistic and achievable.

In order to reach your savings goals, you may need to adjust your spending habits. Practicing the pay-yourself-first method means making conscious decisions about how and where to spend your money in order to prioritize saving. Understanding the long-term value of saving will help you stay committed to building a secure financial future, especially when you take advantage of the benefits of saving through depository institutions.

10 Reasons Why Saving Money Is Crucial (Even When Borrowing is Easy and Cheap)

With credit cards so accessible, it might seem tempting to buy things on credit and pay later, especially if the payments are manageable. But relying on borrowing can have long-term consequences, and many people are falling into this trap. Here are 10 reasons why saving money is essential:

1. **Achieve Financial Independence** Financial independence often means having enough savings to make life choices without relying on a paycheck. This could mean taking a break from work, switching careers, starting a business, or even retiring early. While not the same as being "rich," financial independence gives you the freedom to live on your own terms. Savings are key to achieving this independence.

2. **Save More and Spend Less** Using credit cards without paying them off each month leads to paying more for everything due to high-interest charges. By saving for purchases ahead of time, you avoid this extra cost. Additionally, savings allow you to take advantage of sales and bulk-buying opportunities, potentially saving 24% annually on groceries alone.

3. **Buy a Home** To buy a home, you'll need a down payment, typically 5% of the home's price. You can't borrow this amount from a lender, so saving is essential. Beyond the down payment, there are additional costs to cover, such as closing fees. Savings make homeownership a reality.

4. **Buy a Car** When purchasing a car, a down payment is usually required to get a loan with a reasonable interest rate. While credit cards or financing options may seem like quick solutions, they often come with high-interest rates. By saving up for a larger down payment, you reduce the total cost of the car in the long run.

5. **Get Out of Debt** To break free from debt, you need to start saving. If you continuously use credit cards for emergencies, you'll never be able to pay them off. A good rule is to save at least $500 to $1,000 for emergencies. This reserve fund will allow you to avoid further debt when unexpected expenses arise.

6. **Prepare for Annual Expenses** To avoid relying on credit, save in advance for regular annual costs like vacations, gifts, home repairs, and property taxes. Saving for these expenses ahead of time can alleviate stress and prevent putting them on credit cards.

7. **Cover Unforeseen Expenses** Life is unpredictable. Car repairs, home maintenance, or even unexpected medical bills can arise without warning. Having savings set aside for these unforeseen expenses prevents you from relying on loans or credit cards to cover them.

8. **Handle Emergencies** Emergencies such as accidents, medical issues, or unexpected travel can be costly. Having savings in place gives you peace of mind and the ability to handle these situations without going into debt.

9. **Prepare for Job Loss or Injury** Job security isn't guaranteed, and unforeseen events like job loss or injury can disrupt your income. Employment insurance doesn't kick in immediately, so having savings to fall back on can prevent you from sinking deeper into debt while you recover.

10. **Enjoy a Better Life** Living paycheck to paycheck creates constant stress. People without financial plans often find themselves in crisis mode, constantly reacting to situations. Saving money gives you control over your future, reducing anxiety and helping you live a more stable and fulfilling life.

By saving, you invest in your peace of mind, future security, and happiness. The effort to save today will pay off in a more comfortable, stress-free tomorrow.

Begin Building Your Emergency Savings Fund Today

Start putting aside a small portion of your income with each paycheck until you accumulate an emergency savings fund of $500 to $1,000. If you receive a bonus or a tax refund, consider using that money to kickstart or add to your fund. Life is unpredictable, and you might need to dip into this fund from time to time, but make it a habit to replenish it once you do. While it requires some effort, establishing this habit is crucial for financial stability. You may want to create a budget to help you stay on track.

What Is an Emergency Fund?

An emergency fund is money set aside specifically for unexpected events, such as a car accident, medical emergency, or home repairs. The purpose of this fund is simple: life can throw curveballs, and it's better to be prepared. Having an emergency fund ensures that you're not caught off guard by an unplanned event. Whether it's losing a job or dealing with a sudden repair, this fund provides a financial cushion to handle life's surprises.

How Much Should My Emergency Fund Be?

If you have consumer debt, start by saving a small emergency fund of at least $1,000. Once you're debt-free, focus on building a more robust emergency fund that covers three to six months of living expenses.

The ideal size of your emergency fund depends on your personal circumstances. Generally, if your income is stable, or if you're in a two-income household, a three-month reserve is usually sufficient. However, if you're the sole income earner, self-employed, or work on commission, aim for a six-month cushion to protect against potential income loss.

Additionally, if anyone in your household has ongoing medical needs or frequent doctor visits, a six-month fund is advisable to ensure you're prepared for unforeseen medical expenses, even if your budget can currently accommodate the regular costs. This fund is all about giving you peace of mind, knowing you're financially prepared for whatever life throws your way.

Where Should I Keep My Emergency Fund?

Your emergency savings should be easily accessible, but not so easy that you're tempted to use it for non-emergencies. Here are some good options for where to keep your emergency fund:

- A basic savings account linked to your checking account.
- A money market account that offers the convenience of check-writing or a debit card.
- An online bank account that pays a higher interest rate, allows for quick and direct transfers to your checking account.

The key is to ensure you can quickly access the money when needed, without delays or complications. However, it's important not to keep your emergency fund in an account that's too accessible. For example, my husband and I use a separate bank for our emergency savings to reduce the temptation to dip into it whenever we feel like it.

When Should I Use My Emergency Fund?

Not every unexpected expense is an emergency. Here are three questions to help you determine whether it's time to use your emergency fund:

1. Was it unexpected?
2. Is it necessary?
3. Is it urgent?

If you answer "yes" to most of these questions, then it's likely a true emergency, and using your emergency savings is justified.

How to Build Your Emergency Fund

Building your emergency fund provides peace of mind and financial security. Here's a step-by-step guide to help you get started:

1. **Create a Budget and Stick to It** A budget doesn't restrict you; it shows you what you *can* do. List all your monthly income and expenses so you can see how much you have available to contribute to your emergency fund. This will help you determine the right amount to save.

2. **Set a Monthly Savings Goal** Decide how much you want to set aside each month for your emergency savings. I understand that saving can feel tough, especially when you're used to spending, but you'd be surprised at how quickly your savings can grow if you stay consistent. If you're unsure how much to save, revisit your budget and adjust accordingly.

3. **Adjust Your Savings Amount** Over time, you might find you're able to save even more. If you or your partner get a raise, take advantage of that extra income by adding it to your savings. Regularly review your budget to find new ways to cut costs and boost your savings.

4. **Set Realistic Goals** Start small with a savings goal that feels manageable, and gradually increase it as you pay off debt or improve your financial situation.

Quick Ways to Boost Your Emergency Fund

One of the easiest ways to quickly build up your emergency fund is by selling things you no longer need. Take a look around your garage, attic, or closet—there are likely items collecting dust that could be turned into cash. Selling these things can have a surprising impact on your savings. Even small amounts—$5 here, $10 there—can add up faster than you think.

And don't forget the power of extra work. Consider taking on a part-time job, starting a side hustle, or offering services like dog walking or babysitting. These small efforts can bring in extra cash that will help grow your emergency fund in no time!

Start Your Emergency Fund Today

Take a moment to imagine what life would be like with no debt payments and a fully stocked emergency fund with six months' worth of expenses. Just picture it. Doesn't it feel good to imagine the peace of mind that would come with having that financial safety net in place? An emergency fund acts like insurance—it requires an initial investment, but it covers you when unexpected events happen.

Now that you have that vision, it's time to start working on your emergency fund. Create a budget, focus on paying off any debt, and begin setting aside savings. You'll be amazed at how quickly your emergency fund grows when you're not tied down by debt payments! The best part? You'll experience a newfound sense of security. When life's little hiccups—like a leaky roof or a broken washing machine—happen, you'll find yourself thinking, "Eh, no big deal." That's the peace of mind a fully-funded emergency fund can give you.

To save money fast, you need a plan. Isn't it time to start yours?

Keep the Momentum Going

Once you've started building your emergency fund, the key to success is consistency. Keep adding to it regularly, even if it's just a small amount. Over time, those contributions will accumulate into something substantial. Celebrate the small wins along the way—every step you take brings you closer to that feeling of financial security.

Also, make sure you're setting realistic milestones for yourself. If your goal is to save six months' worth of expenses, break it down into manageable chunks. Don't let the total amount overwhelm you. Instead, focus on what you can save each month, and adjust as needed. If you can afford more, great! If not, just keep plugging away. The most important thing is to stay committed.

Stay Focused on Your Goal

While it's tempting to dip into your emergency fund for non-emergencies, remember the purpose of this fund: to provide financial security during unexpected situations. When considering whether to tap into it, ask yourself the three critical questions:

1. Is it unexpected?
2. Is it necessary?
3. Is it urgent?

If you answer "yes" to all three, it's likely time to use your emergency savings. But for regular, planned expenses, it's better to stick to your budget and save for those separately. The goal is to keep your emergency fund intact for true emergencies.

The Bottom Line

Starting and growing your emergency fund is one of the smartest financial moves you can make. It might feel daunting at first, but once you get the ball rolling, it becomes easier. Plus, the peace of mind you'll gain from having that cushion is priceless.

Remember: you're not just saving for the "what-ifs" of life—you're preparing for the certainty that life will throw challenges your way. By planning ahead and building your emergency fund now, you're setting yourself up for financial stability, no matter what comes next.

How to Find the Best Savings Option:

Finding the best savings option requires evaluating various financial institutions, savings products, and interest rates. It's important to align your savings needs (whether short-term or long-term) with the best tools that offer flexibility, high returns, and low fees.

Here's how to find the best savings option:

1. **Set Your Savings Goals:**

○ **Short-Term Goals**: For goals you plan to achieve in the near future (e.g., building an emergency fund), you'll want to prioritize liquidity and safety. A high-yield savings account or a money market account might be ideal.

○ **Long-Term Goals**: For savings goals that are several years away (e.g., retirement or buying a home), you may want to look into options that offer higher returns, such as certificates of deposit (CDs) or investment accounts.

2. **Research Available Savings Tools:** There are various savings tools designed for different needs. Some may offer better returns, while others might provide more flexibility.

Savings Tools in the Market:

1. **High-Yield Savings Accounts:**

   ○ High-yield savings accounts offer better interest rates than traditional savings accounts. They are typically offered by online banks and may have higher minimum deposit requirements, but they are a safe and liquid way to grow your savings.

   ○ **Pros**: Safety (FDIC-insured), high interest rates, easy access to funds.

   ○ **Cons**: May have minimum balance requirements or fees for falling below the threshold.

2. **Money Market Accounts:**

   ○ Money market accounts are similar to high-yield savings accounts, but they often come with higher minimum deposit requirements and may allow limited check-writing abilities.

   ○ **Pros**: Higher interest rates than traditional savings, often includes limited check-writing.

   ○ **Cons**: Higher minimum balance requirements.

3. **Certificates of Deposit (CDs):**

   ○ A CD is a savings tool where you deposit a fixed amount for a fixed period (e.g., 6 months, 1 year, 5 years), and in return, you get a guaranteed interest rate.

   ○ **Pros**: Guaranteed returns, higher interest rates than savings accounts or money markets, low risk.

   ○ **Cons**: Lack of liquidity (penalties for early withdrawal), fixed rates that might not keep up with inflation.

4. **Treasury Securities:**

   ○ U.S. Treasury bonds, bills, and notes are government-issued securities that offer a fixed return over time. They can be a good option for long-term savings, and they are backed by the U.S. government.

- **Pros**: Low risk, fixed returns, no state or local taxes on interest.
- **Cons**: Low interest rates compared to other tools.

5. **Cash Management Accounts (CMAs):**

- Offered by brokerage firms, CMAs typically combine features of checking, savings, and investment accounts, offering high interest rates and easy access to funds.
- **Pros**: High interest rates, flexibility, low fees.
- **Cons**: Not always FDIC-insured (though some firms offer FDIC coverage through partnering banks).

6. **Roth IRAs and Traditional IRAs (for retirement savings):**

- If you are saving for retirement, IRAs provide tax advantages. Roth IRAs grow tax-free, and Traditional IRAs offer tax-deferred growth.
- **Pros**: Tax advantages, flexibility (for Roth IRAs), wide variety of investments.
- **Cons**: Penalties for early withdrawals (except for specific conditions), contribution limits.

How to Shop for a Financial Institution:

Shopping for a financial institution is crucial to finding the best savings option for your needs. The right institution will provide competitive rates, low fees, and a range of tools that align with your goals.

1. **Evaluate the Reputation:**

- Look for institutions that are well-established and have a solid reputation for customer service. Online reviews and consumer protection websites can provide insights into the customer experience.

○ Ensure that the financial institution is **FDIC-insured** (for savings accounts, checking accounts, and CDs) or **NCUA-insured** (for credit unions), which means your deposits are protected up to $250,000 per depositor, per institution.

2. **Consider the Account Fees:**

○ Look for accounts that offer low or no monthly maintenance fees. Some institutions charge fees if you fall below a certain balance or for certain services (e.g., wire transfers or overdrafts).

○ Compare account fees across institutions to ensure you're not paying unnecessary charges.

3. **Examine the Tools and Services Offered:**

○ Some institutions offer a wide variety of services like automatic transfers, goal-setting tools, or mobile apps that make managing your savings easier. Look for features that suit your lifestyle and savings habits.

4. **Consider Accessibility:**

○ Check whether the institution has physical branches near you (if that's important) or if it operates solely online. Many online banks offer high-yield savings accounts but have limited physical locations, while traditional banks may offer both.

○ Consider online and mobile banking options for ease of access and monitoring your savings.

5. **Look at Minimum Deposit Requirements:**

○ Some accounts require a large initial deposit to open, while others have low or no minimum balance requirements. Make sure the requirements align with your financial situation.

How to Shop for the Best Rate Available in the Market:

1. **Use Comparison Websites:**

○ Websites like **Bankrate**, **NerdWallet**, and **MagnifyMoney** offer easy-to-use comparison tools that allow you to compare savings account rates, CD rates, and other financial products side-by-side. These platforms are regularly updated to show the best rates available across different financial institutions.

2. **Check Promotional Offers:**

○ Financial institutions may offer special promotions with higher interest rates to attract new customers. Look out for limited-time offers on high-yield savings accounts or CDs. Compare these rates to see if they're worth the potential restrictions (e.g., minimum deposits or time limits).

3. **Monitor Interest Rate Trends:**

○ Interest rates can fluctuate based on market conditions and central bank policies. Keep an eye on changes in interest rates from the Federal Reserve, as these influence rates at banks. If you notice a rise in interest rates, it may be a good time to lock in a higher rate on a CD or savings account.

4. **Consider Online Banks:**

○ Online banks tend to offer higher interest rates on savings accounts compared to traditional brick-and-mortar banks. This is because they have lower overhead costs and pass the savings onto customers in the form of higher rates.

5. **Ask for Rate Matching:**

○ If you find a higher rate from a competitor, some financial institutions may be willing to match or beat the rate. This can be particularly true for larger institutions or those trying to retain your business.

Conclusion:

Finding the best savings option involves defining your goals, comparing financial institutions, and selecting the tool that offers the best rate, flexibility, and features to meet your needs. Consider various savings options like high-yield savings accounts, money market accounts, and CDs, and look for financial institutions with a solid reputation, low fees, and high interest rates.

Use comparison websites to shop for the best rates, and don’t hesitate to negotiate for better terms or ask about special promotions. Finally, remember that the best savings option will align with your financial goals, whether you're saving for short-term needs or building wealth for the future.

Chapter 6
Retirement Planning

Initiating Your Retirement Strategy

Many people recognize the need to plan for retirement, yet they may worry about not having saved enough. Rather than feeling overwhelmed by these concerns, it can be helpful to begin by organizing your financial picture and understanding your current retirement resources.

Establishing the Basics

Begin by reviewing all your retirement accounts—including any 401(k) plans from previous employers that haven't yet been consolidated. By gathering and possibly rolling over these accounts into a current 401(k) or an IRA, you gain a clearer view of your overall savings. Even small amounts can accumulate significantly over time.

If you fall on the lower end of the income spectrum, you might be eligible for a savings tax credit for the first $2,000 saved each year. This government incentive can enhance your retirement resources without additional cost.

Utilizing Employer Contributions

Many employers provide access to retirement plans, such as 401(k) plans for private-sector workers, 403(b) accounts for employees in certain public or tax-exempt organizations, and 457 plans for government employees. If your plan offers a matching contribution, consider contributing at least the amount required to receive the full match. (If your employer-sponsored plan has higher fees than other available options, you may wish to contribute only enough to obtain the match and explore lower-fee alternatives for additional savings.)

Self-employed individuals have options as well, such as SEP-IRAs, which are designed to accommodate variable income and offer flexible contribution rules.

Exploring Investment Options

After consolidating existing accounts and taking advantage of employer-sponsored contributions, you might consider additional retirement vehicles. For many, this decision comes down to choosing between a traditional IRA and a Roth IRA (or a SEP-IRA for those who are self-employed).

- **Roth IRA**: Contributions are made with after-tax dollars, so qualified withdrawals during retirement are tax-free.
- **Traditional IRA**: Contributions are made with pre-tax dollars, allowing for tax-deferred growth, though withdrawals in retirement are taxed as ordinary income.

A key consideration is whether your current tax bracket is expected to be higher or lower than what it might be during retirement. This analysis, along with the tax treatment of any other retirement accounts you hold, can help determine the most appropriate option.

Preserving Your Savings

Generally, withdrawing funds from a 401(k) or a traditional IRA before age 59½ results in a 10% early withdrawal penalty (with a few specific exceptions, such as for qualified medical or educational expenses). Maintaining funds within these accounts allows them to continue growing over time.

Adjusting Your Investment Approach as Retirement Nears

Many individuals choose a glide path strategy—also known as target date investing—as they near retirement. With this approach, the investment mix gradually shifts from higher-risk (stocks) to lower-risk (bonds) assets. This change can help reduce volatility; however, with increasing longevity, some investors may wish to maintain a portion of their portfolio in growth-oriented assets even in later years.

Your strategy for converting retirement savings into income will depend on several factors, including your desired spending level, investment growth, inflation, and regulatory requirements. For instance, traditional IRAs require minimum withdrawals (RMDs) beginning at age 70½, whereas Roth IRAs do not have this requirement.

Comprehensive Retirement Planning

Effective retirement planning goes beyond accumulating savings. It involves:

- **Assessing Future Expenses:** Estimating your retirement living costs—including routine expenses and potential medical needs.

- **Evaluating Asset Allocation:** Selecting a mix of investments that offers the potential to outpace inflation while managing risk.

- **Planning Withdrawals:** Develop a strategy to draw down retirement funds in a way that meets your needs over a potentially long retirement period.

Regularly reviewing your net worth and financial goals can help you adjust your strategy as circumstances change.

Overview of Retirement Plan Options

A wide variety of retirement plans exist to meet different needs, including:

- **Individual Retirement Arrangements (IRAs):** Both traditional and Roth

- **Employer-Sponsored Plans:** Such as 401(k), Simple 401(k), 403(b), SIMPLE IRA, and SEP plans
- **Other Options:** Profit-sharing plans, defined benefit plans, money purchase plans, Employee Stock Ownership Plans (ESOPs), governmental plans, and 457 plans.

When comparing plans, consider factors such as tax implications, fees, flexibility, and the specific rules that apply to each option.

Choosing Between Traditional and Roth IRAs

Selecting the right type of IRA involves comparing the tax implications of each:

- **Roth IRA:** Contributions are taxed now; withdrawals in retirement are tax-free.
- **Traditional IRA:** Contributions reduce your taxable income today, but withdrawals are taxed later.

Consider your current and future tax situations, along with your overall retirement strategy, to h Both traditional and Roth IRAs offer the potential for tax-advantaged growth that may help enhance your retirement savings. The primary difference between these options is how contributions and withdrawals are treated for tax purposes.

Traditional IRA

Contributions to a traditional IRA may be partially or fully tax-deductible if your modified adjusted gross income (MAGI) falls below certain thresholds. This deduction can reduce your current taxable income, and taxes on the deductible portion, and any earnings are deferred until you begin withdrawals in retirement. For specific eligibility details and deduction amounts, please refer to IRS.gov or consult a tax advisor.

Roth IRA

Contributions to a Roth IRA are made with after-tax dollars, meaning they are not tax-deductible. In return, qualified withdrawals during retirement are generally tax-free. Regardless of which IRA you choose, you typically have until the federal income tax return filing deadline (excluding extensions) to contribute for the previous tax year. For example, for the 2021 tax year, you could contribute to a Roth IRA if your MAGI was below $140,000 (or $208,000 for married couples filing jointly).

How Tax Considerations Might Influence Your Choice

The tax treatment of these accounts suggests that a traditional IRA might be more suitable if you expect to be in a lower tax bracket during retirement, while a Roth IRA could be a better match if you anticipate a higher tax bracket later on. Additionally, if there is a possibility that you might need to access your funds before age 59½, a Roth IRA may offer more flexibility. Under certain conditions, contributions to a Roth IRA can be withdrawn at any time without triggering taxes or penalties; however, the earnings generally remain subject to tax and penalties unless the withdrawal is qualified. With a traditional IRA, early withdrawals before age 59½ typically incur both income taxes and a 10% penalty, unless an exception applies.

Required Minimum Distributions (RMDs)

Another important difference is that traditional IRAs require you to begin taking RMDs starting at age 72, with these distributions taxed as ordinary income. Roth IRAs do not have RMD requirements for the original account owner, which might be advantageous if you plan to allow the account to continue growing or intend to pass it on to your heirs.

Before deciding on an IRA, it's important to understand all the tax implications and how they align with your personal financial situation. Consulting with a financial advisor or tax specialist can help ensure that you choose the option that best meets your retirement goals.

Help determine which option aligns best with your needs.

Overview of 401(k) Plans

A 401(k) is a component of a qualified profit-sharing plan that permits employees to allocate a portion of their wages into individual retirement accounts. Key characteristics include:

- **Elective Salary Deferrals:** Employees may choose to defer a portion of their wages. These deferred amounts are generally excluded from taxable income at the time of deferral (with the exception of designated Roth deferrals, which are taxed in the year they are made).
- **Employer Contributions:** Employers may also contribute to these individual accounts, subject to applicable plan rules.
- **Taxation of Distributions:** When funds, including earnings, are eventually withdrawn (typically during retirement), they are included in taxable income. However, qualified distributions from designated Roth accounts are treated differently.

A 401(k) plan is structured as a qualified plan, which can be integrated into various types of retirement arrangements, such as profit-sharing, stock bonus plans, pre-ERISA money purchase pension plans, or rural cooperative plans. In these plans, elective deferrals are not subject to federal income tax withholding at the time they are made, and they are not reported as taxable income on the employee's annual income tax return.

Roth Elective Deferrals

Certain 401(k) plans offer employees the option to designate some or all of their elective deferrals as Roth contributions. In this case, these contributions are included in taxable income in the year they are made, following similar tax treatment to that of a Roth IRA.

Tax Advantages

Two notable tax advantages associated with sponsoring a 401(k) plan include:

- **Employer Deductibility:** Employer contributions may be deductible on the employer's federal income tax return, provided they do not exceed limits set forth in section 404 of the Internal Revenue Code. (For more details on these limitations, refer to IRS Publication 560, Retirement Plans for Small Business.)

- **Tax-Deferred Growth:** Elective deferrals and investment gains within the plan are not taxed until they are distributed, allowing for the potential of compounded, tax-deferred growth over time.

Types of 401(k) Plans

Employers have a choice among several types of 401(k) plans, each with its own set of rules:

- **Traditional 401(k) Plans:**
    - Allow eligible employees to make pre-tax elective deferrals via payroll deductions.
    - May include employer contributions, either as a matching component or as non-elective contributions made for all participants.
    - Contributions and employer matches may be subject to a vesting schedule, meaning full ownership of employer contributions is earned over time.
    - Must satisfy nondiscrimination requirements, with annual tests (such as the Actual Deferral Percentage and Actual Contribution Percentage tests) ensuring that benefits do not favor highly compensated employees.

- **Safe Harbor 401(k) Plans:**
    - Similar to traditional plans, they require employer contributions to be fully vested when made.

- Employer contributions can be structured either as matching contributions for employees who defer or as contributions for all eligible employees, regardless of deferrals.
- Are not subject to the complex annual nondiscrimination tests that traditional plans must complete.
- If no additional contributions are made in a year, safe harbor plans may be exempt from certain top-heavy rules.
- Require employers to provide timely written notice to each eligible employee, outlining the plan's features and their rights under the plan.

- **SIMPLE 401(k) Plans:**
  - Designed for small businesses, allowing employers with 100 or fewer employees (each earning at least $5,000 in the preceding calendar year) to offer a cost-effective retirement savings option.
  - Do not require annual nondiscrimination testing.
  - Mandate that employer contributions are fully vested.
  - Typically, employees participating in a SIMPLE 401(k) plan are not eligible for contributions or benefits under any other employer-sponsored retirement plan.

For additional details on the traditional, safe harbor, and SIMPLE 401(k) plans, refer to IRS Publication 4222, 401(k) Plans for Small Businesses.

Participation and Enrollment

Service Requirement: A 401(k) plan generally cannot require employees to complete more than one year of service before becoming eligible to participate.

- **Automatic Enrollment:** Some 401(k) plans feature automatic enrollment. Under this arrangement, a fixed percentage or amount is automatically deducted from an employee's wages and contributed to the 401(k) plan, unless the employee opts out or chooses a different deferral rate. These amounts are treated as elective deferrals.

Each plan must be administered according to the specific rules and qualification requirements established under the tax law to retain its tax-favored status. It is important for employers to be well-informed about these rules so that the plan is managed in compliance with the applicable requirements.

Elective Deferral Limits

Under IRC section 402(g), there is a limit on the amount a participant may defer on a pre-tax basis each year. Any elective deferrals that exceed this limit—or that are recharacterized as after-tax contributions when correcting for nondiscrimination test issues—are included in the employee's gross income.

Matching Contributions

If the plan permits, an employer may make matching contributions based on an employee's elective deferrals. For example, a plan might specify that the employer contributes 50 cents for each dollar deferred by the employee. These matching contributions are subject to nondiscrimination tests to ensure compliance with applicable rules.

Other Employer Contributions

In addition to matching contributions, a plan may allow an employer to make additional contributions on behalf of participants—even for those who do not make elective deferrals. In cases where the plan is determined to be top-heavy (typically when the account balances of key employees exceed 60% of the balances of all participants), the employer may be required to make minimum contributions for certain employees. For further details on determining whether a plan is top-heavy, refer to section 1.416-1 of the Income Tax Regulations.

Employee Compensation Considerations

For example, in 2021, only up to $290,000 of an employee's compensation (with previous limits being $285,000 in 2020 and $280,000 in 2019) may be taken into account when calculating contributions. This limit is adjusted for inflation.

Vesting Requirements

Employees are always fully vested in their own elective deferrals. However, a plan may impose a vesting schedule for employer contributions, meaning that full ownership of those contributions is earned over a specified period of service. For instance, a plan might require the completion of two years of service for an initial percentage of vesting, with additional service required to increase that percentage.

Distributions

Distribution rules determine when a plan may or must provide benefits to participants. For more detailed information on the tax treatment and timing of retirement plan distributions, consult IRS Publication 575, Pension and Annuity Income.

Additional Tax-Advantaged Savings Vehicles

403(b) and 457(b) Plans

- **403(b) Plans:** Also known as tax-sheltered annuity (TSA) plans, these are offered primarily by public schools and certain 501(c)(3) tax-exempt organizations. Employees save for retirement by contributing to individual accounts, and employers may also contribute.

- **457(b) Plans:** These plans, which allow employees to defer income taxation on contributions, are available for certain state and local government employees as well as employees of tax-exempt organizations. Employers or employees through salary reduction can contribute up to the limit specified under IRC section 402(g) (for example, $19,500 in 2021). Detailed information is available on IRS.gov.

Both of these vehicles provide tax deferral on contributions and earnings, allowing retirement savings to potentially grow over time.

Financial Considerations as Retirement Approaches

Recognizing that retirement planning evolves over time, the following checklists provide a framework for assessing financial readiness at different stages before retirement:

One Year Out from Retirement

- **Review and Document Your Retirement Budget:** Prepare a detailed budget that reflects anticipated changes in expenses once you leave full-time employment. Consider that some expenses may decrease while others (such as travel or healthcare) might become more prominent.
- **Test Your Budget:** Consider living on your planned budget for a trial period to assess its feasibility. Minor adjustments may be necessary if shortfalls occur.
- **Develop a Withdrawal Strategy:** Establish a plan for drawing down retirement funds. One common approach is to withdraw approximately 4% of your savings each year, adjusting the dollar amount for inflation.
- **Rebalance Your Investment Portfolio:** Evaluate your asset allocation to ensure it aligns with your time horizon and risk tolerance as you approach retirement.
- **Review Healthcare Coverage:** Examine your Medicare options (for instance, signing up for Medicare Part A when eligible) and consider any outstanding dental or other medical needs.
- **Plan for Future Work Arrangements:** If you expect to work part-time or transition gradually into retirement, discuss potential phased retirement options with your employer.

Five Years Out from Retirement

- **Increase Cash Reserves:** Given that accessing retirement funds may involve processing delays, consider maintaining an emergency fund that could cover three to six months of living expenses.
- **Assess Your Investment Strategy:** It might be appropriate to rebalance your portfolio to a more conservative mix in anticipation of retirement.
- **Consult a Financial Planner:** Meeting with a certified financial planner can provide personalized guidance on tax planning and help refine your retirement strategy.
- **Address Large Expenses:** Plan for major expenses—such as home repairs or vehicle replacements—that may be more manageable to address before transitioning to retirement.
- **Evaluate Retirement Location Options:** If relocating is under consideration, spending extended periods in potential retirement sites can help assess both lifestyle and long-term costs.
- **Consider Professional Certification:** For those who may pursue a second career or part-time work post-retirement, obtaining necessary certifications in advance may prove beneficial.

Ten Years Out from Retirement

- **Begin Outlining Your Retirement Budget:** Even with a decade ahead, formulating a preliminary budget can highlight areas for increased savings or expense reduction.
- **Maximize Contributions:** Take full advantage of tax-advantaged savings opportunities, including catch-up contributions available to those aged 50 and above.
- **Consider a Roth IRA:** Opening a Roth IRA may provide flexibility for emergency needs in retirement, as funds already contributed can generally be accessed without penalty.

- **Review Health Savings Account (HSA) Options:** Contributions to HSAs offer multiple tax benefits—pre-tax contributions, tax-free growth, and tax-free withdrawals for qualified medical expenses—which may be valuable as part of a broader retirement strategy.

- **Maximizing Your Health Savings Account Contributions**: Contributing to a Health Savings Account (HSA) can offer significant tax benefits in three ways. First, you contribute with pre-tax dollars; second, any earnings on your contributions grow tax-free; and third, withdrawals used for qualified medical expenses are not taxed. Since qualified expenses cover a broad range—from basic health items to certain alternative treatments—an HSA can serve as a valuable resource for managing anticipated healthcare costs in retirement.

- **Consider a "Plan B" Career:** Even if you currently enjoy your job, it can be prudent to prepare for the possibility of a career change in the later stages of your working life. Changes in the job market, evolving workplace dynamics, or personal factors such as burnout may prompt you to explore alternative career paths. Researching and considering a backup career plan can help ensure that you have additional options should your current role become less viable over time.

How to Find the Best Savings Option for Retirement Planning?

When planning for retirement, finding the best savings options is critical for ensuring you have sufficient funds to live comfortably in your later years. Unlike regular savings for short-term goals, retirement planning requires careful attention to long-term growth, tax implications, and the need to generate income during retirement.

Here's how you can identify the best savings options for retirement:

1. Understand Your Retirement Goals:

Before selecting any retirement savings tool, it's important to have a clear picture of your retirement goals. Consider factors like:

- **When do you plan to retire?**
- **What kind of lifestyle do you want in retirement?**
- **How much do you expect to spend annually in retirement?**
- **Do you have any other sources of retirement income (e.g., Social Security, pensions)?**

The clearer you are about your goals, the easier it will be to select the right tools for saving.

2. Determine the Time Horizon:

Your time horizon plays a key role in determining the best savings options for retirement. The longer your retirement horizon, the more flexibility you'll have in terms of investment risk.

- **Short-Term Retirement (Less Than 10 Years)**: If you're nearing retirement, you'll want more conservative options that protect your savings, like **high-yield savings accounts** or **CDs**. These accounts offer stability and less risk to your principal but usually lower returns.

- **Long-Term Retirement (More Than 10-20 Years)**: If you're far from retirement, you can afford to take on more risk in exchange for higher returns. This could include **IRAs** (Individual Retirement Accounts), **401(k)** accounts, or **Roth IRAs** that invest in stocks, bonds, mutual funds, or ETFs.

Savings Tools for Retirement Planning:

Here are some common retirement savings tools you should consider:

3. Employer-Sponsored Retirement Plans (401(k), 403(b)):

- **401(k) Plans** (for private sector employees) and **403(b) Plans** (for public sector employees) are the most common retirement savings plans offered by employers. Contributions are made through payroll deductions, and employers may match a portion of your contributions, which is essentially "free money."

○ **Pros**: Tax-deferred growth, employer match, contribution limits are higher than IRAs.

○ **Cons**: Investment options can be limited to what your employer offers, early withdrawals (before age 59½) may incur penalties and taxes.

- **Contribution Limits**: In 2025, employees can contribute up to $22,500 annually to a 401(k), with an additional $7,500 catch-up contribution if over the age of 50. Employer contributions do not count toward this limit.

4. Individual Retirement Accounts (IRAs)

- **Traditional IRAs** allow you to contribute pre-tax dollars, meaning your contributions reduce your taxable income for the year. Your investments grow tax-deferred until you start withdrawing in retirement, at which point the withdrawals are taxed as ordinary income.

- **Roth IRAs** offer tax-free growth. You contribute after-tax dollars, but your withdrawals in retirement (including both principal and earnings) are tax-free, as long as certain conditions are met.

○ **Pros**: Tax advantages (tax-deferred for Traditional IRAs, tax-free for Roth IRAs), flexibility in investment choices (stocks, bonds, mutual funds).

○ **Cons**: Contribution limits. You must meet certain income qualifications for Roth IRAs, and early withdrawals may be penalized.

- **Contribution Limits**: For 2025, the contribution limit for both Traditional and Roth IRAs is $6,500 ($7,500 if you're 50 or older).

5. Health Savings Accounts (HSAs)

Although designed for healthcare savings, **HSAs** are a great retirement planning tool for those with high-deductible health plans (HDHPs). Contributions are tax-deductible, grow tax-deferred, and can be withdrawn tax-free for qualified medical expenses. After age 65, you can withdraw funds for any purpose without penalty (though they will be taxed if not used for healthcare expenses).

- **Pros**: Triple tax advantage (tax-deductible contributions, tax-free growth, tax-free withdrawals for medical expenses), can be used as a supplemental retirement savings account for healthcare.

- **Cons**: You must have a qualifying HDHP to be eligible to contribute.

- **Contribution Limits**: In 2025, the contribution limit is $3,850 for individuals and $7,750 for families, with a $1,000 catch-up contribution for those 55 or older.

6. Annuities (Fixed, Variable, and Immediate Annuities)

An **annuity** is a financial product that provides regular payments for a specified period, typically starting at retirement. Annuities can be a good option for guaranteed income during retirement, but they come with a range of options and fees.

- **Fixed Annuities** provide a guaranteed income for a set period or for life, but typically have lower returns.

- **Variable Annuities** allow you to invest in mutual funds or other securities, and the income varies based on the performance of those investments.

- **Immediate Annuities** start paying out income immediately after you purchase the annuity, while **deferred annuities** delay payouts until a future date.

- **Pros**: Predictable income, can be structured to last your lifetime, can be a good hedge against longevity risk (living too long).**Cons**: High fees, complicated products, less flexibility in withdrawals.

7. Certificates of Deposit (CDs)

CDs are low-risk investments that offer a fixed interest rate for a set period, usually ranging from a few months to several years. They can be a good option for a conservative retirement plan if you don't mind locking up your money for a period.

- **Pros**: Guaranteed returns, low risk, FDIC-insured.
- **Cons**: Early withdrawal penalties, relatively low interest rates.

How to Shop for the Best Rate in Retirement Savings:

1. **Use Comparison Websites**: Websites like **Bankrate**, **NerdWallet**, and **SmartAsset** allow you to compare interest rates, account fees, and terms across various financial institutions. These sites also often provide information about retirement accounts like IRAs and 401(k) plans.

2. **Monitor Federal Reserve Policy**: The **Federal Reserve's interest rate decisions** influence interest rates on savings tools. If the Fed raises rates, savings tools like CDs, money market accounts, and even retirement savings vehicles might offer higher returns.

3. **Check for Employer 401(k) Match**: Always contribute enough to take full advantage of your employer's 401(k) match, as that's essentially free money. After meeting the employer match, you may want to consider opening an IRA or contributing to a Roth IRA to diversify tax benefits.

4. **Look for Low Fees**: Pay attention to the fees associated with each retirement savings tool. High fees can erode the returns on your savings over time, so it's crucial to evaluate any hidden costs, like mutual fund fees or administrative charges in 401(k) plans.

5. How to Shop for the Right Financial Institution for Retirement:

1. **Reputation and Customer Service**: Research the institution's reputation and customer service reviews. Check if they offer tools and resources to help you plan for retirement. Well-established institutions often offer better customer support and financial planning services.

2. **Account Features and Tools**: Make sure the institution offers the tools you need for easy tracking of your retirement savings. Some institutions provide retirement calculators, mobile apps, and educational resources to help you stay on top of your plan.

3. **Consider the Range of Products**: Choose a financial institution that offers a range of retirement products (e.g., 401(k)s, IRAs, annuities, CDs) so you can diversify your retirement savings strategy.

4. **Contribution Matching (for Employer-Sponsored Plans)**: If your employer offers a 401(k) match, make sure you take full advantage of it by contributing enough to meet the match threshold.

Conclusion:

Retirement planning requires thoughtful decisions on which savings tools and financial institutions to choose. Consider your time horizon, risk tolerance, and retirement goals when selecting between options like 401(k)s, IRAs, HSAs, annuities, and CDs. Make sure to research the best rates and products available by using comparison tools and staying informed about market trends and the Federal Reserve's policies.

Start saving early, take advantage of employer matches, and regularly review your retirement plan to ensure you're on track to meet your long-term goals. With the right planning and tools, you can build a secure financial future for your retirement years.

Chapter 7
Youth & Money Management

How to borrow wisely, manage student loan repayments, and explore loan forgiveness programs.

Introducing Your Child to Practical Finance

Money Management for Teens and Their Parents

Teens often face challenges in managing money as they begin to navigate financial independence. With increasing levels of student loans and credit card debt among young adults, developing sound financial habits early on can contribute to a strong financial foundation. Understanding how teens typically spend and save can guide the introduction of age-appropriate money management practices that support long-term financial well-being.

While personal finance isn't always part of the school curriculum, learning about smart spending, saving, and budgeting is valuable for future financial stability. Below are some strategies that may help teens build essential money management skills:

1. Creating a College-Friendly Budget

College expenses can add up quickly—from school supplies and dorm snacks to late-night meals. Developing a budget helps clarify available income (such as financial aid or earnings from part-time work) and outlines expected expenses (including tuition, books, and housing). After covering necessary costs, any remaining funds can be allocated toward savings or discretionary spending. Digital tools and budgeting apps can offer up-to-date insights into spending and saving patterns.

2. Gaining Practical Banking Experience

Opening a checking account can be a practical step toward financial independence. A checking account—with access to a debit card—can help teens learn how to manage their money responsibly. When selecting a bank, it's useful to look for options that provide fee-free access to ATMs near campus and, if available, offer maintenance fee waivers for eligible students.

3. Utilizing Banking Apps

Most banks offer mobile apps that allow users to check account activity, monitor balances, deposit checks remotely, and pay bills from anywhere. These features can make managing finances more convenient, especially for busy college students. If some functions are unclear, exploring local branch services or online tutorials (such as those available on YouTube) can provide additional guidance.

4. Building a Strong Credit History

A solid credit history can ease future processes, such as obtaining an apartment lease, a car loan, or a cellphone plan. Since establishing credit typically requires having some form of credit account, there are several approaches to consider. For instance, a teen might be added as an authorized user on a parent's credit card account. This allows them to make purchases while the primary account holder remains responsible for managing the account. Alternatively, obtaining a secured credit card—which requires a deposit that often matches the credit limit—can offer a controlled environment for learning responsible credit use.

5. Learning Strategies for Smart Credit Card Use

Understanding the fundamentals of credit card usage—including interest rates, fees, and the importance of timely payments—can help lay the groundwork for responsible credit practices. Familiarizing teens with these concepts can support informed financial decision-making.

Maintaining an Ongoing Focus on Financial Planning

Money management is an evolving process, and revisiting financial strategies regularly can help adapt to changing circumstances. Starting to build and refine budgeting, saving, and spending habits at an early age can contribute to a more secure financial future as teens transition into adulthood.

1. Managing Card Usage: For teens who are authorized users on a parent's account, consider establishing clear guidelines for card use. Determine a reasonable monthly spending limit and discuss whether certain purchases should be reviewed beforehand.

For students with their own cards, it is important to understand that imprudent use can negatively affect their credit scores. If a parent or guardian is a cosigner, any misuse could also impact their credit. Emphasize the importance of responsible spending and timely bill payments. For example, starting with one small recurring expense—such as a subscription service—with automatic payments can help build a habit of consistency.

If a teen is an authorized user, periodically monitoring card activity can help ensure that spending remains within the agreed-upon guidelines. Cosigners might consider reviewing account activity at regular intervals, with the student's consent, to promote responsible financial behavior.

2. Utilizing Account Alerts: Encourage teens to sign up for email or text notifications that provide updates on account balances, recent transactions, and upcoming payment due dates. These alerts can help them avoid issues such as overdrawing their account or missing a payment.

3. Using Mobile Payment Apps Wisely: Discuss safe practices when using mobile payment apps like Zelle® and Venmo, which can simplify splitting expenses such as restaurant bills, ride-sharing costs, food deliveries, or rent. It is advisable to verify recipient information carefully before sending funds and to limit transactions to trusted contacts. Keep in mind that multiple small payments can accumulate and affect account balances. For example, Bank of America customers can use Zelle to securely send, request, or receive money with other U.S.-based bank account holders.

4. Highlighting the Benefits of Saving: As financial responsibilities grow, cultivating a habit of saving becomes increasingly important. Encourage teens to set aside funds regularly, even if the amount is small. Saving can be beneficial for unexpected emergencies or for planning for larger future expenses, such as a spring break trip or a new car. Consistent contributions can accumulate over time and foster healthy financial habits.

5. Offering Savvy Spending Tips: There are several practical strategies to help manage expenses:

- **Textbooks:** Consider purchasing used textbooks online or exploring rental options.
- **Meal Plans:** Evaluate different meal plan options, as many students opt to dine out instead.
- **Discounts:** Inquire about student discounts on items like electronics, cellphone plans, museum admissions, and more.
- **Apps:** Utilize student-focused apps that highlight deals and exclusive offers.

6. Protecting Personal Information: Due to the unique challenges of shared living spaces and evolving financial habits, it is important for college students to safeguard their personal information:

- **Passwords:** Use unique, confidential passwords, update them regularly, and avoid sharing them.

- **Security Features:** Activate all available security features on financial accounts, such as biometric authentication and two-factor authentication, which adds an extra verification step.

- **Social Security:** Share Social Security numbers only with verified and trusted sources.

- **Avoiding Scams:** Be cautious about opening unsolicited email attachments and learn to recognize suspicious website links. Additionally, consider installing anti-malware software for added protection.

This guidance is intended to provide practical information to help teens and their parents develop effective money management skills, without implying any obligatory commitments beyond building an understanding of responsible financial practices.

Budgeting

Even without a full-time job or a mortgage, basic budgeting skills can be valuable for planning expenses and managing money effectively. Here are six steps to build a simple budget:

1. **Determine Income**: Start by identifying all sources of income. For tweens and teens, this might include earnings from part-time jobs, allowances, or monetary gifts received on birthdays and holidays. Add these amounts together to find the total monthly income.

2. **List Required Expenses**: Identify the regular, necessary costs that must be paid. For a middle or high school student, this might include a monthly cell phone bill or, if applicable, expenses related to driving (like gas and car insurance). Tally these expenses to create a baseline for monthly spending.

3. **Subtract Expenses from Income**: After calculating the required expenses, subtract that total from the monthly income. This calculation shows whether available funds are sufficient for essential costs and indicates any remaining amount.

4. **Consider Discretionary Spending**: Discuss that any funds remaining after covering necessary expenses may be used for discretionary purchases or deposited into a savings account. Explain that spending on non-essential items—such as movie tickets or concert admissions—should be balanced with long-term goals, as choosing one expense over another may involve trade-offs.

5. **Plan for Larger Purchases**: For items that are more expensive, like a bicycle or a car, it can be helpful to set a savings target and develop a plan to reach that goal over time.

6. **Maintain a Balanced Budget**: The guiding principle is that spending should not exceed income. If spending surpasses income, it may be necessary to look for ways to reduce expenses or to generate additional income—such as by taking on extra work like mowing lawns or babysitting.

Saving Money – Short- and Long-Term Goals: Learning to save money is an important step toward developing strong financial habits. A savings account can provide a practical way to start setting aside funds for unexpected expenses or larger future purchases. Below are two common types of accounts that can be considered:

Option 1: Youth Savings Accounts: Youth savings accounts are designed to meet the needs of young savers and often feature:

- Lower minimum balance requirements
- Inexpensive maintenance fees
- Joint ownership, where the account is held in both a parent's and the child's name (since minors generally cannot open bank accounts independently)

- A transfer process to full ownership when the child reaches a specified age

Some banks require a minimum age to open a youth savings account, while others, such as Bank of America, do not impose this restriction. These accounts can be used for managing a portion of monetary gifts or allowances and serve as a practical tool for understanding concepts like interest accrual, fees, and withdrawal limitations (for example, federal law limits certain types of transfers to six per month).

Option 2: Custodial Savings Accounts: Custodial savings accounts, governed by the Uniform Gifts to Minors Act (UGMA) or the Uniform Transfers to Minors Act (UTMA), allow funds to be deposited and managed by an adult custodian while legally belonging to the minor. The minor gains full control of the account once they reach the designated age (usually 18 or 21, depending on local regulations). Funds may be accessed early if they are used directly for the child's benefit, such as covering expenses for summer camp, tutoring, or contributing toward a first car. Custodial accounts can also offer tax benefits on interest income, although contributions above certain thresholds may have gift tax implications. It is advisable to review any tax and financial aid considerations before opening such an account.

Real-Life Lessons: Discussing money management with young people can sometimes be challenging, but practical steps—such as opening a savings account together—can enhance financial understanding. Choosing the appropriate savings account depends on individual goals and circumstances. By exploring these options and discussing them openly, parents and children can work together to build a solid foundation for financial success.

Building and Maintaining a Healthy Credit Score

Your credit score is a key element of your financial profile. It reflects your creditworthiness and plays a major role in determining the terms and costs of any loans you might seek. Typically represented by a FICO score, it indicates how responsibly you manage your finances. A higher score can open doors to lower interest rates, helping you borrow more affordably for both immediate needs and significant long-term investments.

Because missed or late payments on obligations such as a mortgage, auto loans, or credit cards can lower your score, it's important to stay current with all your bills. A weakened credit score can lead to higher borrowing costs and may even impact areas like rental agreements, employment opportunities, or auto insurance rates.

Key factors that influence your credit score include:

- **Payment History:** Consistently paying bills on time is the most critical component. Timely payments on all your credit accounts help build a strong credit record.
- **Amounts Owed:** Keeping your debt levels low relative to your available credit (a lower debt-to-credit ratio) is viewed favorably by lenders.
- **Length of Credit History:** Demonstrating a long, responsible credit history can have a positive impact on your score.
- **Credit Mix:** A diverse range of credit types—such as credit cards, installment loans, and mortgages—shows experience in managing various forms of credit.
- **New Credit:** Frequent applications for new credit can signal financial strain and may temporarily lower your score.

It is wise to review your credit reports from the three major agencies—Experian, TransUnion, and Equifax—at least once a year. You can obtain a free report from each through AnnualCreditReport.com (the reports are free, although obtaining your credit score may involve a fee). Regular reviews help ensure the accuracy of your credit information, and any discrepancies should be addressed promptly.

Overall, maintaining a healthy credit score involves consistently paying your bills on time, managing your debt levels, and being mindful of new credit inquiries.

Planning for College Education Savings

Preparing financially for college requires careful consideration of several factors that determine the total amount needed. Key considerations include:

- **Savings Timeline:** The number of years until your child starts college influences both the amount you need to save and the potential growth of your investments. More time allows for gradual savings accumulation and investment growth.
- **Type of Institution:** Tuition rates can vary widely between public and private colleges. For example, during the 2018–2019 academic year, in-state tuition and fees at public four-year colleges averaged around $10,230, whereas private colleges typically charged significantly more.
- **Special Programs:** If your child is interested in study abroad or summer coursework, additional expenses such as travel, program fees, and extra housing or meal costs should be factored into your savings goal.
- **Advanced Study Requirements:** For careers that require postgraduate education, additional savings will be necessary beyond what is needed for an undergraduate degree.
- **Living Expenses:** Costs such as housing, food, and transportation can vary depending on the college's location. For instance, living expenses in a major city may be considerably higher than those in a rural area where on-campus housing is available.

After evaluating these factors, you can estimate the future cost of college. Keep in mind that expenses are likely to increase over time, so planning well in advance can provide a more accurate savings target.

What Can I Do If I Start Saving for College Late?

If you begin saving for college later than planned, there are several strategies you can consider:

- **Trim Your Budget:** Look for ways to reduce your monthly expenses to free up funds for college savings.

- **Seek Contributions:** Friends and family might be willing to contribute to your child's college fund in lieu of traditional gifts for occasions like birthdays.

- **Consider Alternative Education Paths:** Encourage your teen to explore options such as attending a two-year community college. This route typically offers lower tuition costs, and credits earned may be transferable to a four-year institution later. This approach can help reduce initial tuition expenses, allowing a larger portion of the college fund to potentially grow over time.

How Else Can I Pay for College If I Can't Save Enough?

Families often use multiple resources to cover college expenses. In 2018, for example, about 47 percent of tuition payments came from parent and student income and savings, according to Sallie Mae. Additional sources can include:

- **Scholarships and Grants:** Numerous government and private organizations, as well as the schools themselves, offer scholarships and grants that do not require repayment.

- **Federal and Private Loans:** Low-interest federal student loans, as well as private loans, can help fill any gaps between savings and total costs.

- **Guidance and Local Resources:** High school guidance counselors can provide information about qualifying for aid and local scholarships. Additionally, cultural, professional, religious organizations and even some employers may offer financial assistance.

Tip: To access federal aid—which in 2018 included nearly $120 billion in grants, work-study funds, and low-interest loans—it is essential to complete the Free Application for Federal Student Aid (FAFSA).

What Is a 529 Plan and How Can It Help with Education Savings?

A 529 education savings plan is a tax-advantaged account designed to help families set aside funds for future education expenses. Key features include:

- **Tax-Free Growth:** Investments in a 529 plan grow without being subject to federal taxes.
- **Tax-Free Withdrawals:** When funds are used for qualified higher education expenses—such as tuition, room and board, computers, and books—withdrawals (including earnings) are not taxed.
- **Investment Options:** These plans typically offer a variety of investment choices.

Important Note: As with any investment, the value of a 529 plan can fluctuate, and there is a risk of loss. Some states also offer tax deductions for contributions made to in-state 529 plans, so it is advisable to check with your state before selecting a plan.

Planning for College: Understanding Costs and Financial Aid

Preparing for college involves considering both the total cost of attendance and the net price you will actually pay after financial aid.

- **Total Cost of Attendance:** This includes tuition, fees, room and board, books and supplies, transportation, and other expenses such as extracurricular activities.
- **Net Price:** This is the total cost minus any grant aid and scholarships. It does not include loans, which must be repaid later.

For the 2024–2025 academic year, the average published tuition and fees are:

- **Public Two-Year Colleges (In-District):** $4,050 per year. research.collegeboard.org
- **Public Four-Year Universities (In-State):** $11,610 per year. research.collegeboard.org
- **Private Four-Year Universities:** $43,505 per year. usnews.com

It's important to note that these figures represent the "sticker price" and do not account for financial aid, scholarships, or grants, which can significantly reduce the actual cost to families. The net price, which is the amount students and families typically pay after financial aid, is often lower. For instance, in 2024–2025, the average net price for public two-year colleges was $2,480, and for public four-year institutions, it was $16,510. nasfaa.org

Over the past decade, the cost of attending public universities has decreased significantly when adjusted for inflation. The average tuition for in-state public universities has dropped by 4%, and the net cost after financial aid has decreased by 40%, from $4,140 to $2,480 annually. apnews.com

Many colleges provide net price calculators on their websites to help families estimate what they might pay after financial aid. These calculators take into account your family's financial information to estimate an "expected family contribution" (EFC). The EFC is then subtracted from the college's published cost of attendance to determine your financial need.

Tip: Since financial aid packages can vary widely between schools, it is a good idea to submit the FAFSA as early as possible. FAFSA applications typically become available in January of the year your child will attend college, and the application must be updated each subsequent year.

Managing Student Loans

Understanding the basics of student loans can be helpful as you plan for college expenses:

1. **FAFSA:** The Free Application for Federal Student Aid is required to qualify for federal benefits such as grants, work-study programs, and student loans.

2. **Principal and Interest:** The principal is the amount borrowed, and the interest is the fee charged by the lender, calculated as a percentage of the principal. Federal student loan interest rates are set by Congress, while private loan rates vary based on factors like credit history and loan terms. Lower interest rates generally result in lower overall repayment costs.

3. **Federal Student Loans:** These loans typically offer more favorable terms than private loans, including fixed interest rates and income-driven repayment options.

By combining savings with financial aid, scholarships, and, if necessary, student loans, you can develop a comprehensive strategy for funding college education.

With this information, you and your family can explore various strategies and resources for funding college, enabling you to make informed decisions based on your financial situation and educational goals.

These reductions are attributed to tuition freezes during the COVID-19 pandemic and increased state and federal funding. Despite these trends, it's essential to research individual institutions, as costs can vary widely.

Federal student loans are financial aid provided by the U.S. Department of Education to help students cover the costs of higher education. These loans typically offer lower interest rates and more flexible repayment options compared to private loans. The primary types of federal student loans available include:

1. **Direct Subsidized Loans**: These are need-based loans for undergraduate students. The government pays the interest while you're in school at least half-time, during the grace period, and during deferment periods.

2. **Direct Unsubsidized Loans**: Available to both undergraduate and graduate students, these loans are not based on financial need. Interest accrues during all periods, including while you're in school and during deferment or forbearance periods.

3. **Direct PLUS Loans**: These loans are for graduate or professional students and parents of dependent undergraduate students. A credit check is required, and interest accrues during all periods.

4. **Direct Consolidation Loans**: This option allows you to combine multiple federal student loans into a single loan with a fixed interest rate, simplifying repayment.

For more detailed information on these loan types, you can visit the Federal Student Aid website. studentaid.gov

In terms of repayment options, the Department of Education offers various plans to accommodate different financial situations. These include standard repayment plans with fixed monthly payments over a set period, graduated repayment plans with payments that start lower and increase over time, and income-driven repayment plans that base your monthly payment on your income and family size. It's important to choose a repayment plan that aligns with your financial circumstances to manage your debt effectively.

Recent developments have introduced changes to repayment plans. The Saving on a Valuable Education (SAVE) Plan, an income-driven repayment plan, was created to offer lower monthly payments and prevent loan balances from growing, provided borrowers make their required payments. However, parts of the SAVE Plan have been temporarily blocked by court orders, leading to some uncertainty. studentloanborrowerassistance.org

Additionally, the Department of Education has placed borrowers enrolled in the SAVE Plan into forbearance due to ongoing litigation and system updates. During this forbearance, which is expected to last until at least September 2025, borrowers are not required to make payments, and interest is not accruing. However, this period does not count toward forgiveness programs like Public Service Loan Forgiveness (PSLF) or income-driven repayment forgiveness. ed.gov

Given these evolving circumstances, it's crucial to stay informed about the latest updates from the Department of Education and to consult with your loan servicer to understand how these changes may affect your repayment strategy.

Chapter 8
Smart Taxes

Being smart about taxes involves understanding the system, taking advantage of opportunities for tax savings, and planning ahead. Here are six ways to be strategic about taxes:

1. Understand Tax Brackets and Rates

- **What It Is:** The U.S. tax system operates on a progressive scale, where income is taxed at different rates depending on the amount. There are multiple tax brackets, with higher income levels taxed at higher rates.
- **How to Be Smart:** By understanding where your income falls within these brackets, you can make decisions that help minimize your tax liability. For example, you may consider timing certain income or deductions to ensure you're in a lower bracket or utilize tax-efficient investment strategies like tax-deferred accounts.

2. Maximize Tax-Advantaged Accounts

- **What It Is:** Tax-advantaged accounts allow you to save money and reduce your taxable income. Common examples include 401(k)s, IRAs, and Health Savings Accounts (HSAs).
- **How to Be Smart:** Contribute as much as possible to these accounts, as they can help lower your taxable income. For example, contributions to a traditional 401(k) or IRA are tax-

deductible, reducing your tax burden for the year you contribute. For HSAs, the contributions are deductible, and the funds can be used tax-free for qualified medical expenses. Moreover, taking full advantage of your employer's matching contributions (for retirement accounts) is essentially "free money."

3. Take Advantage of Tax Credits

- **What It Is:** Tax credits directly reduce the amount of tax you owe, unlike deductions which reduce your taxable income. There are a variety of tax credits, such as the Child Tax Credit, Earned Income Tax Credit (EITC), and education credits like the American Opportunity Credit.
- **How to Be Smart:** Identify the credits you qualify for and claim them on your tax return. Credits are typically more valuable than deductions because they directly reduce your tax bill. For instance, the Child Tax Credit can provide up to $2,000 per qualifying child, and the Earned Income Tax Credit can provide significant savings for low-to-moderate-income earners.

4. Use Tax Deductions Wisely

- **What It Is:** Deductions reduce your taxable income. Common deductions include those for mortgage interest, charitable contributions, state and local taxes, and student loan interest.
- **How to Be Smart:** Keep track of all potential deductions throughout the year, and itemize them if they exceed the standard deduction for your filing status. For instance, if you donate to charity, keep receipts or records. Additionally, if you have a home office for work, you may qualify for the home office deduction. Being organized with your deductions can result in a lower taxable income and a smaller tax bill.

5. Consider Tax-Efficient Investments

- **What It Is:** Some investments are more tax-efficient than others. For example, qualified dividends, long-term capital gains, and municipal bonds often have favorable tax treatment.

- **How to Be Smart:** Invest in assets that minimize tax exposure. For example, municipal bonds are generally exempt from federal taxes and sometimes state and local taxes. Also, consider holding investments in tax-advantaged accounts (like an IRA or 401(k)) so that their growth is sheltered from taxes. If you're invested in taxable accounts, be mindful of tax-efficient funds, such as index funds, which tend to have lower capital gains distributions.

6. Plan for Tax Changes and Future Years

- **What It Is:** Tax laws can change annually, so it's important to stay updated on new tax regulations. Additionally, planning for taxes in future years is critical, especially if you expect changes in income or deductions.

- **How to Be Smart:** Make adjustments as needed. For example, if you expect a significant increase in income in the next year (e.g., a raise, bonus, or new job), you might want to consider shifting some income or deductions to the current year to take advantage of lower tax rates. You should also consult a tax professional if significant tax law changes occur, as this can help you adjust your tax strategy. Planning ahead, whether for retirement or a big purchase, can ensure you're maximizing your tax situation over time.

By understanding and strategically applying these six points, you can significantly reduce your tax burden, optimize your finances, and take control of your financial future.

Simple tax strategies to minimize tax liability and maximize deductions.

Here are some simple, effective tax strategies you can use to minimize your tax liability and maximize your deductions:

1. Contribute to Retirement Accounts

- **What It Is:** Contributing to tax-deferred retirement accounts like a 401(k), traditional IRA, or 403(b) can reduce your taxable income in the year you make the contribution.

- **How It Helps:** Contributions to traditional retirement accounts are generally tax-deductible, meaning the money you contribute will not be taxed until you withdraw it in retirement. This can reduce your taxable income, potentially lowering your overall tax liability. For example, if you contribute $5,000 to your 401(k), your taxable income for the year is reduced by $5,000.

- **Additional Tip:** Maximize your contributions to take full advantage of tax-deferred growth. For 2025, the contribution limit for a 401(k) is $22,500 ($30,000 for those over 50), and for IRAs, the limit is $6,500 ($7,500 for those over 50).

2. Take Advantage of Tax Deductions

- **What It Is:** Deductions lower your taxable income, reducing the amount of tax you owe. The most common deductions include mortgage interest, student loan interest, state and local taxes (SALT), and charitable contributions.

- **How It Helps:** Keep track of all deductible expenses throughout the year, such as donations to qualified charities or business expenses if you're self-employed. You can either take the standard deduction or itemize your deductions if they exceed the standard amount. For 2025, the standard deduction for single filers is $13,850 and $27,700 for married couples filing jointly.

- **Additional Tip:** If you're close to the standard deduction threshold, consider bunching deductions into one year (such as making multiple charitable donations in one year) to exceed the threshold and itemize your deductions.

3. Maximize Contributions to Health Savings Accounts (HSAs)

- **What It Is:** An HSA allows you to set aside pre-tax money for medical expenses, and any unused funds roll over from year to year.

- **How It Helps:** Contributions to an HSA are tax-deductible, and the money in the account grows tax-free. You can also withdraw the funds tax-free for qualified medical expenses. This strategy is especially helpful for those with high-deductible health plans (HDHPs). In 2025, the contribution limits for HSAs are $3,850 for individual coverage and $7,750 for family coverage.

- **Additional Tip:** If you're over 55, you can make an additional catch-up contribution of $1,000, which increases your annual limit and allows you to save even more on taxes.

4. Use Tax Loss Harvesting

- **What It Is:** Tax loss harvesting is a strategy in which you sell investments at a loss to offset capital gains.

- **How It Helps:** If you have investments that have lost value, you can sell them to create a capital loss. This loss can offset any capital gains you've realized from other investments, reducing your taxable income. If your losses exceed your gains, you can use up to $3,000 of the excess loss to offset other income, such as wages.

- **Additional Tip:** Be mindful of the "wash sale" rule, which prevents you from claiming a loss if you buy the same or substantially identical security within 30 days of selling it at a loss.

5. Claim Dependent Deductions and Credits

- **What It Is:** If you have children or dependents, there are several tax credits and deductions available to reduce your tax burden.

- **How It Helps:** The Child Tax Credit, for instance, provides up to $2,000 per child (under age 17) for qualifying taxpayers, which directly reduces the amount of tax owed. Additionally, you can claim deductions for childcare expenses, education costs, and even for taking care of elderly parents in some situations.

- **Additional Tip:** If you're eligible, be sure to also claim the Child and Dependent Care Credit or the Earned Income Tax Credit (EITC), which can offer significant savings for low-to-moderate-income families.

6. Consider a Tax-Deferred Investment Strategy

- **What It Is:** Tax-deferred accounts allow your investments to grow without being taxed until you withdraw the funds.

- **How It Helps:** Contributing to accounts like a 401(k) or a traditional IRA allows your investments to grow tax-deferred, meaning you won't pay taxes on the earnings until you take the money out in retirement. This can be especially helpful for long-term savings, as it allows your investments to compound without the drag of taxes.

- **Additional Tip:** If you're self-employed, you might also consider setting up a SEP IRA or solo 401(k), which has higher contribution limits than traditional IRAs.

7. Utilize the Standard Mileage Rate for Business Expenses

- **What It Is:** If you use your car for business purposes, you can deduct the mileage driven.

- **How It Helps:** The IRS provides a standard mileage rate that you can use to calculate your business-related mileage deductions. This is a great way to reduce your taxable income if you're self-employed or run a small business. For 2025, the IRS standard mileage rate is 65.5 cents per mile.

- **Additional Tip:** Keep accurate records of your mileage and the purpose of each trip. If you drive a lot for work, this could add up to significant deductions.

8. Take Advantage of Education-Related Tax Benefits

- **What It Is:** There are several tax breaks available for those paying for education, either for themselves or their children.

- **How It Helps:** The American Opportunity Tax Credit (AOTC) provides up to $2,500 per year for each eligible student for the first four years of post-secondary education. The Lifetime

Learning Credit offers up to $2,000 per tax return for qualified education expenses. You can also deduct student loan interest (up to $2,500 per year).

- **Additional Tip:** Keep all receipts for qualified education expenses and tuition payments, as these will be necessary to claim these benefits.

Yes! Here are a few more strategies to minimize tax liability and maximize deductions:

9. Claim the Qualified Business Income Deduction (QBI)

- **What It Is:** The Qualified Business Income (QBI) deduction allows business owners to deduct up to 20% of their qualified business income from a pass-through entity, such as a sole proprietorship, S-corp, or partnership.

- **How It Helps:** This deduction can significantly reduce taxable income for eligible business owners. It's available to those with businesses that qualify as "pass-through" entities, and the deduction is typically available to individuals with taxable income below $429,800 (for married filing jointly) or $214,900 (for single filers) in 2025.

- **Additional Tip:** Make sure to track all eligible business income and expenses, and consult a tax advisor if you are unsure whether your business qualifies for the QBI deduction.

10. Deduct Home Office Expenses

- **What It Is:** If you work from home, you may qualify to deduct some of your home office expenses, such as utilities, internet, and office supplies.

- **How It Helps:** For the home office deduction, you can either use the simplified method (which offers a deduction of $5 per square foot up to 300 square feet) or the actual expense method, which requires calculating the percentage of your home used for business and deducting related expenses (mortgage interest, utilities, repairs, etc.).

- **Additional Tip:** Keep in mind that the IRS has strict guidelines regarding the home office deduction; the space must be used exclusively for business purposes.

11. Take Advantage of Energy-Efficient Tax Credits

- **What It Is:** There are tax credits available for making your home more energy-efficient, such as installing solar panels, energy-efficient windows, or geothermal heat pumps.
- **How It Helps:** The Residential Energy Efficient Property Credit allows you to claim up to 26% of the cost of installing solar panels or other renewable energy systems in your home. This can reduce your tax liability significantly. Similarly, the Nonbusiness Energy Property Credit allows you to claim a portion of the costs of improving your home's energy efficiency.
- **Additional Tip:** Check with your tax professional to ensure you qualify for these credits and that you're maximizing the savings from any energy-efficient upgrades.

12. Plan for Capital Gains

- **What It Is:** Capital gains taxes are taxes on the profit from the sale of assets like stocks, bonds, or real estate. Long-term capital gains (on assets held longer than one year) are taxed at a lower rate than short-term capital gains.
- **How It Helps:** To reduce taxes on capital gains, hold investments for more than one year to benefit from the long-term capital gains tax rate, which is generally lower. Additionally, offset any capital gains with capital losses through tax loss harvesting.
- **Additional Tip:** If you're in a lower tax bracket, you may qualify for 0% capital gains tax on long-term investments. Be sure to review your income and investment situation before making sales.

13. Take Advantage of the Child Tax Credit and Other Family Credits

- **What It Is:** The Child Tax Credit (CTC) and the Credit for Other Dependents (ODC) are available for families with children and other dependents. The CTC provides up to $2,000 per qualifying child, while the ODC offers $500 for dependents who don't qualify for the CTC (such as older children or non-child dependents).
- **How It Helps:** These credits directly reduce your tax liability, and in some cases, you may receive a refund even if your liability is less than the credit amount (this is called a refundable credit). In 2025, the CTC is fully refundable for families with earned income over $2,500.
- **Additional Tip:** Ensure that your children or dependents meet all the eligibility requirements to qualify for these credits and consult a tax professional if you have complex family circumstances.

14. Use Flexible Spending Accounts (FSAs)

- **What It Is:** A Flexible Spending Account (FSA) allows you to set aside pre-tax dollars for eligible expenses such as medical bills, child care, and dependent care.
- **How It Helps:** Contributions to an FSA are tax-free, reducing your taxable income. This means you pay less in taxes while saving for healthcare or dependent care expenses. In 2025, the contribution limit for health FSAs is $3,050.
- **Additional Tip:** Be mindful that FSAs typically have a "use-it-or-lose-it" policy, meaning you must use the funds within the year or risk losing them. Make sure you plan your contributions wisely.

15. Defer Income Where Possible

- **What It Is:** Deferring income means postponing receipt of income to a future year. This is commonly done through retirement accounts or if you have control over the timing of bonuses or other types of income.

- **How It Helps:** If you anticipate being in a lower tax bracket in the following year, deferring income can help lower your taxable income for the current year and reduce your overall tax liability. You can also defer income by contributing to tax-deferred retirement accounts, which delays tax payments until retirement.

- **Additional Tip:** If you have flexibility in when you receive a bonus or other income, consider asking your employer to delay payment until the next tax year if doing so would place you in a lower tax bracket.

16. Donate to Charity

- **What It Is:** Charitable donations are a great way to reduce your tax liability while giving back to your community. Both cash and property donations can be deducted, as long as the charity is qualified.

- **How It Helps:** You can deduct your charitable contributions if you itemize your deductions. This lowers your taxable income and can reduce the amount of taxes you owe. For donations of property, the deduction is based on the fair market value of the item.

- **Additional Tip:** Keep receipts and documentation for all donations, and if donating large items like furniture or real estate, make sure to have an appraisal to verify the value of the donation.

17. Claim the Adoption Credit

- **What It Is:** If you adopt a child, you may be eligible for the Adoption Tax Credit, which can provide up to $15,000 in tax credits for qualified adoption expenses.

- **How It Helps:** The credit can be claimed for adoption-related expenses such as adoption fees, attorney fees, and court costs. It directly reduces your tax liability on a dollar-for-dollar basis.

- **Additional Tip:** The credit is non-refundable, meaning it can reduce your tax liability to zero, but not result in a refund. Keep all receipts for adoption-related expenses to ensure you're claiming the maximum credit.

Yes, there are several more tax strategies that can help you minimize your tax liability and maximize your deductions. Here are additional strategies to consider:

18. Maximize Retirement Contributions

- **What It Is:** Contributions to retirement accounts, such as a 401(k), Traditional IRA, or SEP IRA, are tax-deferred, meaning you won't pay taxes on the amount contributed until you withdraw the money in retirement.

- **How It Helps:** By contributing the maximum allowable amount to these accounts, you lower your taxable income in the current year. This can lead to a significant reduction in your tax bill. For example, in 2025, the 401(k) contribution limit is $22,500 (or $30,000 if you're 50 or older), and for IRAs, the limit is $6,500 (or $7,500 if you're 50 or older).

- **Additional Tip:** Take advantage of employer matching contributions to your 401(k) if available, as this is essentially "free" money for your retirement.

19. Consider a Roth IRA Conversion

- **What It Is:** A Roth IRA conversion involves moving funds from a Traditional IRA or 401(k) to a Roth IRA. While you must pay taxes on the amount you convert, future withdrawals from a Roth IRA are tax-free.

- **How It Helps:** If you anticipate being in a higher tax bracket in retirement, converting to a Roth IRA may make sense. It allows for tax-free withdrawals in the future, and it can also help reduce your required minimum distributions (RMDs) in retirement, as Roth IRAs do not require RMDs.

- **Additional Tip:** Consider converting during years when your income is lower or when tax rates are more favorable. You can also spread the conversion over several years to avoid a large tax bill all at once.

20. Leverage the Lifetime Learning Credit and American Opportunity Credit

- **What It Is:** The Lifetime Learning Credit provides up to $2,000 per year for qualified educational expenses, and the American Opportunity Credit offers up to $2,500 for the first four years of post-secondary education.

- **How It Helps:** These education credits directly reduce your tax liability and can be especially valuable if you or your dependents are pursuing higher education. Unlike deductions, these credits reduce your tax bill on a dollar-for-dollar basis.

- **Additional Tip:** Make sure to check the eligibility criteria, such as the type of institution and the taxpayer's income level, to ensure you qualify for these credits.

21. Use a Health Savings Account (HSA)

- **What It Is:** A Health Savings Account (HSA) allows you to set aside money tax-free for qualified medical expenses. To contribute to an HSA, you must be enrolled in a high-deductible health plan (HDHP).

- **How It Helps:** Contributions to an HSA are tax-deductible, and withdrawals for qualified medical expenses are tax-free. This can lower your taxable income and provide tax-free benefits for healthcare costs. Additionally, unused HSA funds roll over year after year, and after age 65, you can use the funds for any purpose without penalty (though non-medical withdrawals are subject to income tax).

- **Additional Tip:** Contributing the maximum amount to your HSA each year can be a great way to save for future healthcare costs while reducing your current tax liability.

22. Claim the Saver's Credit

- **What It Is:** The Saver's Credit, also known as the Retirement Savings Contributions Credit, is a tax credit for eligible low- to moderate-income individuals who contribute to a retirement account, such as a 401(k) or IRA.

- **How It Helps:** This credit can provide up to $1,000 ($2,000 for married couples filing jointly) in tax savings, in addition to the tax deduction you already receive for retirement contributions.

- **Additional Tip:** The credit is based on both your contribution to the retirement account and your income level. The lower your income and the higher your contribution, the more significant the credit you can claim.

23. Take Advantage of Depreciation on Rental Properties

- **What It Is:** If you own rental property, you can deduct depreciation on the property to reduce taxable income. Depreciation is a non-cash expense that allows you to deduct the cost of the property over time.

- **How It Helps:** By claiming depreciation, you can reduce your taxable rental income, which could result in lower taxes. The IRS allows you to depreciate rental properties over 27.5 years for residential properties.

- **Additional Tip:** Keep track of all property improvements and maintenance costs, as these may also be deductible, further reducing your taxable income.

24. Utilize the Capital Gains Tax Exclusion for Home Sales

- **What It Is:** When you sell your primary residence, you can exclude up to $250,000 ($500,000 for married couples filing jointly) of capital gains if you meet specific ownership and use tests.

- **How It Helps:** This exclusion can help reduce or eliminate taxes on the sale of your home. If your home has appreciated significantly in value since you purchased it, this could be a substantial tax savings.
- **Additional Tip:** Ensure you meet the eligibility requirements, such as living in the home for at least two of the last five years before the sale.

25. Defer Taxes on Stock Options

- **What It Is:** If you have stock options from your employer, consider deferring them if possible. Stock options can create tax liabilities when exercised, but there may be strategies to delay taxes.
- **How It Helps:** By exercising options in a tax-efficient way, such as by holding onto the stock for more than one year to benefit from long-term capital gains treatment, you can minimize taxes. Alternatively, you can defer the exercise of options to a future year when your income may be lower.
- **Additional Tip:** Consult with a financial planner to help you understand the best strategy for exercising stock options based on your financial situation.

26. Use Tax-Advantaged Accounts for Education Savings (529 Plans)

- **What It Is:** A 529 plan allows you to save for education expenses in a tax-advantaged account. Contributions are made with after-tax dollars, but the money grows tax-deferred, and withdrawals for qualified educational expenses are tax-free.
- **How It Helps:** This strategy allows you to save for your child's education while reducing the tax impact on your savings. Some states also offer state income tax deductions for contributions to a 529 plan.

- **Additional Tip:** 529 plans can be used for a wide range of education expenses, including K-12 tuition (up to $10,000 per year), college, and even some apprenticeship programs.

27. Track Business Expenses (for the Self-Employed)

- **What It Is:** If you are self-employed or own a small business, you can deduct business expenses to reduce your taxable income. This includes costs related to operating your business, such as office supplies, travel, marketing, and home office expenses.

- **How It Helps:** By deducting legitimate business expenses, you can significantly reduce your taxable income, which lowers the taxes owed on your business earnings.

- **Additional Tip:** Maintain detailed records of all business expenses and keep receipts. Make sure to distinguish between personal and business expenses to avoid issues with the IRS.

These strategies, when combined with previous ones, can greatly enhance your ability to reduce your tax liability. As always, it's wise to consult a tax professional who can help ensure that you're taking full advantage of all available tax-saving opportunities based on your specific situation.

By incorporating these additional strategies, you can further reduce your tax liability and ensure you're making the most of the available deductions and credits. Always stay up-to-date with tax laws, and when in doubt, consult with a tax professional to make sure you're on the right track.

By applying these simple tax strategies, you can minimize your tax liability, reduce your taxable income, and potentially increase your refund. Regularly review your financial situation, stay updated on any tax law changes, and plan ahead to ensure you're making the most of these strategies.

8.2 Tax Credits Explained-

A **tax credit** is an amount of money that taxpayers can subtract directly from the taxes they owe to the government. It reduces your overall tax liability, dollar for dollar. Unlike tax deductions, which reduce your taxable income, tax credits directly lower the amount of taxes you need to pay. This makes tax credits one of the most powerful tools for reducing taxes.

Types of Tax Credits

There are two primary types of tax credits: **nonrefundable** and **refundable**.

1. Nonrefundable Tax Credit

- **What It Is:** A nonrefundable tax credit allows you to reduce your tax liability to zero but not below zero. In other words, if your tax liability is less than the amount of the credit, you will lose the difference.

- **Example:** If you owe $500 in taxes but have a $600 nonrefundable credit, your tax liability will be reduced to zero, but the remaining $100 of the credit will not be refunded to you.

2. Refundable Tax Credit

- **What It Is:** A refundable tax credit allows you to reduce your tax liability to zero, and if there is any remaining credit, you will receive the balance as a refund. This means you can receive a refund even if your tax liability is less than the value of the credit.

- **Example:** If you owe $500 in taxes and have a $600 refundable tax credit, your tax liability will be reduced to zero, and you will receive a refund of the remaining $100.

How Tax Credits Work

The process for claiming a tax credit is relatively simple:

1. **Eligibility:** To claim a tax credit, you must meet certain eligibility requirements, which could include income limits, filing status, or other conditions depending on the credit.

2. **Claiming the Credit:** You will report your eligible tax credits on your tax return. Specific forms or schedules are used for different types of credits.

3. **Reduction of Tax Liability:** Once your eligibility is confirmed, the tax credit is applied directly to your tax liability, reducing the amount you owe.

Examples of Common Tax Credits

Here are some common types of tax credits available to individuals and businesses:

1. Earned Income Tax Credit (EITC)

- **What It Is:** The Earned Income Tax Credit is a refundable credit designed to help low- to moderate-income working individuals and families. The amount of the credit varies based on income, filing status, and number of dependents.
- **Benefit:** The EITC can provide a significant financial boost, especially for families with children.

2. Child Tax Credit

- **What It Is:** The Child Tax Credit is available to taxpayers with qualifying children under the age of 17. As of 2025, taxpayers may receive up to $2,000 per child, with up to $1,500 being potentially refundable.
- **Benefit:** This credit can reduce your tax liability significantly, and if you don't owe enough taxes, you may receive part of the credit as a refund.

3. American Opportunity Tax Credit (AOTC)

- **What It Is:** The AOTC is a partially refundable tax credit for qualified education expenses for students in their first four years of higher education. It allows a credit of up to $2,500 per eligible student, with up to $1,000 being refundable.

- **Benefit:** This credit can help offset the cost of tuition, fees, and course materials.

4. Lifetime Learning Credit (LLC)

- **What It Is:** The LLC is a nonrefundable tax credit that provides up to $2,000 per tax return for qualified education expenses. Unlike the AOTC, it is available for all years of post-secondary education.

- **Benefit:** This credit helps offset the costs of tuition, books, and other educational supplies.

5. Energy-Efficient Home Improvement Credit

- **What It Is:** The Energy Efficient Home Improvement Credit is a tax credit for taxpayers who make qualified energy-efficient improvements to their homes, such as installing solar panels, windows, or insulation.

- **Benefit:** This credit can reduce the upfront costs of energy-efficient home upgrades and lower your tax liability.

6. Adoption Credit

- **What It Is:** The adoption tax credit provides a credit for qualified adoption expenses, including adoption fees, court costs, and other adoption-related expenses.

- **Benefit:** This is a nonrefundable credit that helps offset the costs of adopting a child.

Differences Between Tax Credit and Tax Deduction

It's important to distinguish between tax credits and tax deductions:

- **Tax Credits:** Directly reduce your tax liability. The more credits you qualify for, the less you'll owe (or the more you may receive if the credit is refundable).

- **Tax Deductions:** Reduce your taxable income, meaning you pay taxes on a smaller amount of income. While they can lower your tax liability, the reduction is not as direct as a tax credit. The amount you save depends on your tax bracket.

Tax Credit vs. Tax Refund

- **Tax Credit:** Reduces your tax liability by the value of the credit.
- **Tax Refund:** If you've overpaid taxes during the year, you might receive a refund when you file your tax return. A refund is the amount of tax you paid in excess of your actual liability.

Strategic Use of Tax Credits

- **Maximizing Credits:** Tax credits are a valuable tool for reducing your tax bill, so it's crucial to explore all the credits you may be eligible for.
- **Refundable Credits:** These are particularly advantageous because they can result in a refund even if you don't owe any taxes.

Claiming Multiple Credits: In some cases, you can claim more than one credit, depending on your situation (e.g., both the Child Tax Credit and the Earned Income Tax Credit).

How to Claim Tax Credits?

To claim a tax credit, you generally need to follow these steps:

1. **Determine Eligibility:** Each tax credit has specific eligibility criteria. Review these to ensure you qualify. Some credits may require specific documentation, such as proof of education expenses or adoption costs.
2. **Gather Necessary Documentation:** Collect all the required documentation to support your claim. This could include receipts, tax forms (e.g., Form 8862 for the Earned Income Tax Credit), and other evidence of eligibility.

3. **Complete the Correct Forms:** To claim a tax credit, you'll need to fill out specific forms. For example, if you're claiming the Child Tax Credit, you'll need to complete Schedule 8812. Other credits will require different forms (e.g., Form 8863 for education credits).

4. **Submit the Tax Return:** Once you've completed the required forms and verified that you qualify, file your tax return, either electronically or by mail. If you're claiming multiple credits, ensure that everything is accounted for.

5. **Monitor the Processing of Your Return:** After submitting your tax return, you may need to follow up if there are any issues or discrepancies. Keep an eye on the status of your return and any communication from the IRS.

Impact of Tax Credits on Your Financial Planning

Tax credits can be a powerful tool in your financial planning, offering both immediate relief and long-term benefits. Here's how to think about them as part of your overall financial strategy:

1. Minimize Tax Liability Efficiently

- By understanding and utilizing available tax credits, you can reduce your tax liability in a straightforward manner. For example, if you qualify for the Earned Income Tax Credit or Child Tax Credit, you could significantly lower what you owe or even receive a refund.

2. Maximize Refunds

- Refundable credits like the Child Tax Credit and the Earned Income Tax Credit are ideal for maximizing your refund. This could provide additional funds to pay down debt, save for future goals, or invest in other financial strategies.

3. Adjust Withholding or Estimated Payments

- Tax credits might make it possible to adjust your withholding or estimated tax payments throughout the year. If you're expecting a large tax refund due to credits, you might consider adjusting your withholding to keep more of your paycheck throughout the year instead of waiting for a refund.

4. Financial Planning for Future Tax Years

- If you anticipate qualifying for credits in the future (e.g., education credits, home improvement credits, or credits related to family status changes), consider how this might impact your tax strategy going forward. Planning ahead for these potential savings can help you better manage your finances and savings goals.

5. Avoiding Common Pitfalls

- It's crucial to understand the requirements and limits of tax credits to avoid potential mistakes. For example, if you claim a credit you're not eligible for or overestimate your eligibility, it could lead to an audit or fines. Always double-check eligibility before claiming a credit and keep thorough records.

Additional Tax Credit Tips

- **Stay Updated on Tax Law Changes:** Tax credits are subject to change from year to year. For example, Congress might increase the amount of a credit or change eligibility requirements. Make sure to stay informed about any changes to tax laws that could affect your credits.
- **Consult with a Tax Professional:** If you're unsure about your eligibility for certain credits or need help navigating complex tax situations, consulting with a tax professional can be beneficial. They can help ensure you claim all eligible credits and avoid common mistakes.
- **Use Online Tools and Resources:** Many tax preparation websites and tools offer guidance on claiming credits. These tools can help identify credits you might qualify for and make the filing process smoother.

Tax credits are one of the best ways to reduce your tax liability and potentially increase your refund. They come in many forms, from education and child-related credits to credits for energy-efficient home improvements. Understanding how they work and ensuring that you qualify for the credits available to you can make a significant difference in your overall tax situation. Whether you are a low-income worker benefiting from the Earned Income Tax Credit or a homeowner making green upgrades and claiming an energy credit, tax credits offer tangible financial benefits. Always keep track of eligibility criteria and seek professional help when needed to maximize the credits you're entitled to.

Tax credits are an essential part of the tax code that can significantly reduce your tax liability. Understanding which credits, you qualify for and using them effectively is a key strategy in tax planning. Whether you're eligible for education credits, energy-efficient home improvement credits, or family-related credits, knowing your options can make a significant impact on your financial well-being. Always ensure you meet the requirements for each credit and keep up with any changes in tax law that might affect your eligibility.

8.3 Understanding Tax Brackets

How tax brackets work and their impact on taxable income.

What Are Tax Brackets?

A **tax bracket** is a range of income that is taxed at a specific rate. In progressive tax systems, like the one in the United States, the tax rate increases as income rises. Each bracket represents a certain portion of your taxable income, which is taxed at the corresponding rate.

The U.S. federal tax system uses **seven tax brackets**, with different tax rates applied to different ranges of taxable income. Taxable income refers to the amount of income left after all deductions and exemptions have been applied.

Current U.S. Federal Tax Brackets for 2024

For the 2024 tax year (for taxes filed in 2025), the U.S. federal tax brackets for individual taxpayers are as follows:

Tax Rate	For Single Filers	For Married Filing Jointly	For Head of Household
10%	Up to $11,000	Up to $22,000	Up to $15,700
12%	$11,001 to $44,725	$22,001 to $89,450	$15,701 to $59,550
22%	$44,726 to $95,375	$89,451 to $190,750	$59,551 to $95,350
24%	$95,376 to $182,100	$190,751 to $364,200	$95,351 to $182,100
32%	$182,101 to $231,250	$364,201 to $462,500	$182,101 to $231,250
35%	$231,251 to $578,100	$462,501 to $693,750	$231,251 to $578,100
37%	Over $578,101	Over $693,751	Over $578,101

How Tax Brackets Work

Tax brackets are structured progressively. This means that as your income rises, you pay higher taxes on the income that falls into each bracket.

For example:

- If a **single filer** has a taxable income of $50,000, they will pay:
  - **10%** on the first $11,000 of income = $1,100
  - **12%** on the next $33,725 (the income between $11,001 and $44,725) = $4,047
  - **22%** on the remaining $5,275 (the income between $44,726 and $50,000) = $1,160.50

So, the total tax due would be the sum of these amounts: **$1,100 + $4,047 + $1,160.50 = $6,307.50**

The **important takeaway** here is that each portion of your income is taxed at the rate that corresponds to its bracket, not all of your income is taxed at the highest rate. This is why it's a progressive tax system.

Marginal vs. Effective Tax Rate

- **Marginal Tax Rate**: This is the rate at which your last dollar of income is taxed. In the example above, the taxpayer's marginal tax rate is 22%, because that's the rate applied to the last portion of income (between $44,725 and $50,000).
- **Effective Tax Rate**: This is the **average tax rate** you pay on your total income. It is calculated by dividing the total amount of tax you pay by your total taxable income. For the example above:

Effective Tax Rate = Total Tax / Total Taxable Income
Effective Tax Rate = $6,307.50 / $50,000 = 12.6%

Even though the marginal tax rate is 22%, the effective tax rate is much lower because the lower portions of the income are taxed at lower rates.

Tax Brackets and Taxable Income

Your **taxable income** is the portion of your income that is subject to taxation after deductions and exemptions. Here's how tax brackets impact your taxable income:

1. **Deductions**: Deductions lower your taxable income. The most common deductions include the standard deduction (which varies based on filing status) and itemized deductions (such as mortgage interest, medical expenses, etc.). Reducing your taxable income through deductions helps to lower the amount of income that is subject to higher tax brackets.

2. **Taxable Income After Deductions**: Once you've applied deductions (either standard or itemized), the remaining income is your taxable income, which will be subject to the tax brackets.

Example of How Deductions Work:

- Let's say you are a **single filer** with $60,000 in gross income.
- You take the **standard deduction** of $13,850 (for 2024).
- Your **taxable income** would be: **$60,000 (gross income) - $13,850 (standard deduction) = $46,150**.

With a taxable income of $46,150, the individual would pay:

- **10%** on the first $11,000 = $1,100
- **12%** on the next $33,725 = $4,047
- **22%** on the remaining $1,425 (from $44,725 to $46,150) = $313.50

Total tax = **$1,100 + $4,047 + $313.50 = $5,460.50**.

This is how tax brackets apply to taxable income, and deductions help lower the amount of income that falls into higher brackets.

Impact of Tax Brackets on Financial Planning

Understanding tax brackets is crucial for effective financial planning. Here's how tax brackets impact your overall financial situation:

1. **Income Planning**: If you're in a higher tax bracket, you may want to find ways to reduce your taxable income by using retirement accounts (e.g., 401(k), IRA), tax-loss harvesting, or charitable donations. These strategies can help shift your income into lower tax brackets.

2. **Investment Decisions**: Income generated from investments is often taxed differently. For example, long-term capital gains (from investments held for more than a year) are typically taxed

at lower rates than ordinary income. Understanding your tax bracket can guide you in choosing tax-efficient investments.

3. **Timing of Income**: If you are close to a higher tax bracket, deferring income to the next tax year (if possible) could reduce your tax liability for the current year.

Charts for Reference

Example of Tax Bracket Impact on Income

Taxable Income	**Tax Rate**	**Tax Due**
$50,000	22%	$6,307.50
$100,000	24%	$18,407.50
$150,000	32%	$34,657.50
$250,000	35%	$63,407.50

This chart shows how different levels of taxable income are taxed at different rates, and the higher your taxable income, the higher the tax liability in terms of the total amount of tax paid.

Conclusion

Tax brackets are a critical aspect of the U.S. tax system, helping to determine how much you owe based on your taxable income. With progressive rates, your income is taxed in portions according to these brackets. Understanding how they work, and how your deductions affect your taxable income, can lead to better tax planning and help you optimize your tax strategy for financial success. Always remember that tax planning is not just about lowering your taxes today but ensuring that your financial decisions align with long-term goals.

8.4 Types of Tax Deductions

Types of Tax Deductions

Tax deductions reduce your taxable income, which in turn reduces the amount of income subject to tax. Understanding the different types of deductions available can help you minimize your tax liability and potentially increase your tax refund. Below are the main types of tax deductions:

1. Standard Deduction

The **standard deduction** is a fixed amount that reduces the income on which you are taxed. For many taxpayers, this is the simplest and most beneficial option, as it does not require you to itemize specific expenses.

For 2024, the standard deduction amounts are:

- **Single filers**: $13,850
- **Married filing jointly**: $27,700
- **Head of Household**: $20,800

Pros:

- Simple to claim, no need to keep track of receipts or specific expenses.
- It's automatically applied when you file your tax return if you don't itemize deductions.

Cons:

- It may not be the most beneficial option if you have substantial itemizable expenses that exceed the standard deduction threshold.

2. Itemized Deductions

Itemized deductions allow you to deduct specific personal expenses from your taxable income. If your qualifying expenses exceed the standard deduction, you may benefit from itemizing your deductions. Here are common examples:

Common Itemized Deductions:

- **Medical and Dental Expenses**: You can deduct unreimbursed medical and dental expenses that exceed 7.5% of your adjusted gross income (AGI).

Example: If your AGI is $50,000, you can only deduct medical expenses over $3,750.

- **State and Local Taxes (SALT)**: You can deduct up to $10,000 in state and local taxes, including property, income, or sales taxes.
- **Mortgage Interest**: Interest paid on a mortgage for your primary and, in some cases, secondary home can be deducted. You can also deduct interest on home equity loans if the funds were used for home improvements.
- **Charitable Contributions**: Donations to qualified charitable organizations can be deducted. This includes cash donations as well as the fair market value of donated goods.
- **Personal Property Taxes**: You may deduct taxes on personal property, such as vehicles and boats, based on the assessed value.
- **Casualty and Theft Losses**: Losses due to natural disasters or theft may be deductible, but they must meet certain criteria, such as being in a federally declared disaster area.

Pros:

- Can significantly lower your taxable income if your total itemized deductions exceed the standard deduction.
- Provides flexibility for claiming a variety of personal expenses.

Cons:

- Requires keeping detailed records of expenses and receipts.
- The process of itemizing may be time-consuming and complex.

3. Above-the-Line Deductions

Above-the-line deductions are deductions that reduce your taxable income, regardless of whether you take the standard deduction or itemize. These deductions are subtracted from your gross income to calculate your AGI. Below are common examples:

Common Above-the-Line Deductions:

- **Student Loan Interest**: You can deduct up to $2,500 in interest paid on qualifying student loans, subject to income limits.
- **Retirement Contributions**: Contributions to traditional IRAs, 401(k)s, and other retirement plans may be deductible, reducing your taxable income for the year.
- **Self-Employment Expenses**: If you're self-employed, you can deduct business expenses, including office supplies, business-related travel, and home office expenses.
- **Health Savings Account (HSA) Contributions**: Contributions to an HSA are deductible, and the funds grow tax-free if used for qualified medical expenses.
- **Alimony Payments** (for divorces finalized before 2019): Alimony payments made to a former spouse are deductible for the payer.

Pros:

- Reduces taxable income before applying the standard or itemized deduction.
- Can be claimed regardless of whether you itemize or take the standard deduction.

Cons:

- Some deductions have income limits or restrictions.
- For some deductions, you may need to keep track of specific records or documents.

4. Tax Credits for Education

There are several tax deductions and credits available to individuals who pay for education expenses. These credits can directly reduce the amount of tax you owe.

Common Education-Related Deductions and Credits:

- **American Opportunity Tax Credit (AOTC)**: Provides up to $2,500 per student for the first four years of higher education. A portion of this credit is refundable, meaning you may receive money even if you owe no taxes.
- **Lifetime Learning Credit (LLC)**: Offers a credit of up to $2,000 for qualified tuition and related expenses for postsecondary education, including graduate school.
- **Tuition and Fee Deduction**: For certain taxpayers, you can deduct up to $4,000 in tuition and fees paid for higher education. This deduction is phased out at higher income levels.

5. Retirement Account Deductions

Contributions to qualified retirement accounts, such as **401(k)s** or **IRAs**, can often be deducted from your taxable income.

Examples:

- **Traditional IRA Contributions**: You can deduct contributions to a traditional IRA (up to a limit) from your taxable income, potentially reducing your tax liability for the year. The amount you can deduct depends on factors like your income and whether you or your spouse are covered by a workplace retirement plan.

- **401(k) Contributions**: Contributions to employer-sponsored 401(k) retirement plans are deducted from your taxable income, up to the annual limit ($22,500 for 2024, or $30,000 if you're age 50 or older). These deductions lower your taxable income for the current year, while your contributions grow tax-deferred.

6. Child and Dependent Care Expenses

If you pay for child or dependent care in order to work or look for work, you may qualify for tax deductions or credits related to those expenses. The **Child and Dependent Care Credit** can help offset costs for child care, as well as care for a disabled spouse or dependent.

- **Child Tax Credit**: Provides a tax credit of up to $2,000 per qualifying child. The credit phases out at higher income levels.

- **Dependent Care Flexible Spending Accounts (FSAs)**: If your employer offers an FSA, you can contribute pre-tax dollars to pay for eligible child and dependent care expenses. This helps reduce your taxable income.

7. Mortgage Interest Deduction

The mortgage interest deduction allows homeowners to deduct the interest paid on their mortgage loan for a primary or secondary home. For new loans, interest on up to $750,000 of mortgage debt is deductible ($375,000 for married taxpayers filing separately). This deduction can be a substantial benefit for homeowners, especially those with high mortgage balances.

8. Business Deductions for Self-Employed Individuals

If you're self-employed, you can deduct a wide range of business-related expenses to reduce your taxable income. These include:

- **Office Supplies**: Deduct the cost of office supplies like paper, ink, and computers.

- **Home Office Deduction**: If you work from home, you may qualify for a home office deduction, based on the percentage of your home used exclusively for work.
- **Business Travel**: Travel expenses related to business, such as airfare, hotels, and meals, can be deducted.

How they reduce taxes on income

Reducing taxes on your income requires strategic planning and taking advantage of available tax-saving opportunities. Here are several ways to minimize your taxable income and, ultimately, reduce the taxes you owe:

1. Contribute to Tax-Advantaged Retirement Accounts

Contributing to retirement accounts such as 401(k)s, IRAs and other tax-deferred accounts can help reduce your taxable income for the year.

- **401(k)**: Contributions to a traditional 401(k) are made with pre-tax dollars, meaning they are deducted from your taxable income. The contributions grow tax-deferred until withdrawal, usually in retirement.
- **Traditional IRA**: Contributions to a traditional IRA are often deductible from your taxable income, reducing the amount of income that is subject to tax. Keep in mind that there are income limits for deducting IRA contributions if you or your spouse is covered by a retirement plan at work.
- **Roth IRA**: While contributions to a Roth IRA do not reduce your taxable income today, withdrawals in retirement are tax-free. This is especially beneficial if you expect to be in a higher tax bracket in the future.
- **Other Employer-Sponsored Plans**: Contributing to other retirement plans such as 403(b)s or 457(b)s, if available, can also reduce your taxable income.

2. Take Advantage of Tax Credits

Tax credits directly reduce the amount of taxes you owe, rather than just reducing your taxable income. There are numerous credits you can use to reduce your tax bill:

- **Child Tax Credit**: If you have children, you may qualify for the child tax credit, which provides up to $2,000 per child.
- **Earned Income Tax Credit (EITC)**: For low- to moderate-income taxpayers, the EITC can provide a significant refund or reduce the taxes owed.
- **Education Tax Credits**: Credits like the American Opportunity Tax Credit (AOTC) or Lifetime Learning Credit can offset the cost of higher education.
- **Energy-Efficient Home Improvements**: If you make certain energy-efficient home improvements, you may be eligible for tax credits, such as those for installing solar panels or energy-efficient windows.

3. Itemize Deductions

While the standard deduction may be beneficial for many taxpayers, itemizing deductions may provide larger tax savings if you have substantial expenses. Some common deductions include:

- **Mortgage Interest**: If you own a home, the interest paid on your mortgage is tax-deductible.
- **State and Local Taxes (SALT)**: You can deduct up to $10,000 in state and local taxes, including income taxes, property taxes, and sales taxes.
- **Medical Expenses**: If your medical and dental expenses exceed 7.5% of your AGI, you can deduct the excess.

- **Charitable Contributions**: Donations to qualified charitable organizations are deductible, which can reduce your taxable income.

4. Utilize Tax-Advantaged Savings Accounts

Certain types of savings accounts allow you to save for specific purposes with tax benefits:

- **Health Savings Accounts (HSAs)**: Contributions to an HSA are tax-deductible, and withdrawals used for qualified medical expenses are tax-free. This is a great option if you have a high-deductible health plan.
- **Flexible Spending Accounts (FSAs)**: Contributions to an FSA reduce your taxable income. FSAs are often used for medical expenses, dependent care, or commuting costs.
- **529 College Savings Plans**: Contributions to a 529 plan are not deductible on your federal taxes, but the earnings grow tax-free, and withdrawals used for qualified education expenses are also tax-free.

5. Claim Business Deductions (if Self-Employed)

If you are self-employed or run your own business, you can deduct a wide range of expenses that directly relate to your work. These deductions reduce your taxable income, helping you lower your tax bill.

- **Home Office Deduction**: If you work from home, you can claim a portion of your home expenses, such as rent, utilities, and internet, as business expenses.
- **Business Expenses**: Deduct expenses for office supplies, travel, advertising, equipment, and any other expenses necessary for running your business.
- **Self-Employment Tax Deduction**: Self-employed individuals can deduct the employer portion of the self-employment tax from their income.

6. Take Advantage of Capital Gains Tax Rates

Long-term capital gains (for assets held for over a year) are taxed at a lower rate than ordinary income. This can be particularly advantageous for investments such as stocks, bonds, and real estate. To minimize taxes on your capital gains:

- **Hold Investments Longer**: To benefit from lower long-term capital gains rates, hold investments for at least a year before selling.
- **Tax-Loss Harvesting**: Offset gains by selling investments at a loss. The losses can be used to reduce the taxable amount of your gains.

7. Tax-Efficient Investment Strategies

How you invest can affect your tax liability. Consider the following strategies:

- **Invest in Tax-Exempt Bonds**: Interest earned from municipal bonds is typically exempt from federal taxes (and sometimes state taxes), making them a good choice for reducing tax liability.
- **Tax-Deferred Accounts**: Use tax-deferred investment accounts like 401(k)s or IRAs for investing. This way, your earnings grow without being taxed until withdrawal.
- **Dividend Income**: Qualified dividends are generally taxed at a lower rate than ordinary income, so investing in dividend-paying stocks may offer tax advantages.

8. Gift Assets to Reduce Your Estate Tax Exposure

If you're looking to reduce future taxes on your estate, gifting assets to others can lower the size of your taxable estate. There are several strategies for gifting:

- **Annual Gift Exclusion**: You can give up to $17,000 per person (2024 limit) each year without having to pay gift tax.

- **529 Plans**: Contributions to 529 college savings plans for family members can reduce the size of your taxable estate while benefiting future generations.

9. Maximize Deductions for Business or Work-Related Expenses

If you are employed, some of your work-related expenses may be deductible, especially if you're self-employed. For example:

- **Work-related Travel**: Travel expenses for business trips, including lodging, meals, and transportation, are tax-deductible if you're self-employed.
- **Education Expenses**: You may be able to deduct certain educational expenses that improve your job skills, such as tuition or training costs.

10. Defer Income

Defer income to a future year, if possible, to reduce your taxable income for the current year. For instance:

- **401(k) Contributions**: By contributing more to your 401(k) or other retirement accounts, you reduce your taxable income in the current year.
- **Timing Bonuses or Pay Raises**: If you have control over when you receive income, consider deferring bonuses or pay raises to the next year when your tax situation might be more favorable.

Conclusion

To effectively reduce taxes on your income, you need to take advantage of available deductions, credits, and strategies that align with your financial goals. The key is to be proactive—whether through contributing to retirement accounts, claiming business expenses, or using tax-advantaged savings accounts. Each of these strategies can help lower your taxable income and reduce the taxes you owe. However, it's important to consult with a tax professional to determine the best approach based on your unique financial situation.

Tax deductions are powerful tools for reducing your taxable income, thereby lowering the amount of taxes you owe. It's important to understand the various types of deductions available and to choose the ones that will benefit you the most. By keeping track of qualifying expenses, maintaining good records, and understanding the rules for each deduction, you can minimize your tax liability and maximize your potential refund. Consider consulting with a tax professional if you're unsure which deductions are most beneficial for your specific financial situation.

How to Find the Best Tax Advisor for Retirement Planning

When planning for retirement, one of the most important decisions you'll make is choosing a **tax advisor**. A qualified tax advisor can help you navigate complex tax rules, identify strategies to minimize your tax burden, and ensure that your retirement savings grow as efficiently as possible. Here's how to find the right tax advisor and what to consider when shopping for one:

1. Understand the Role of a Tax Advisor:

A tax advisor specializes in advising individuals and businesses on how to manage their taxes and ensure they comply with the law while maximizing financial benefits. In the context of **retirement planning**, a tax advisor will:

- Help you identify tax-efficient ways to save for retirement.
- Advise you on which retirement accounts to contribute to (Traditional IRA, Roth IRA, 401(k), etc.), depending on your tax situation.
- Provide strategies for minimizing taxes on retirement income, including Social Security benefits, pension income, and withdrawals from retirement accounts.

- Ensure you understand how tax law changes might affect your retirement plans, especially in relation to tax rates, tax brackets, and tax-advantaged accounts.
- Assist in planning for tax-efficient withdrawals during retirement.

2. Key Qualities to Look for in a Tax Advisor:

When searching for a tax advisor, consider these factors to ensure you find someone who is qualified and suited to your needs:

- **Credentials**:
    - Look for a tax advisor who holds credentials such as **Certified Public Accountant (CPA)**, **Enrolled Agent (EA)**, or a **tax attorney**. These professionals have passed rigorous exams and have the expertise to provide sound tax advice.
    - If the advisor also specializes in financial planning and retirement, they may hold certifications like **Certified Financial Planner (CFP)** or **Chartered Financial Consultant (ChFC)**, which can be valuable for retirement planning.
- **Experience and Specialization**:
    - Choose an advisor who has experience working with **retirement planning** specifically. They should have an understanding of retirement-specific tax strategies, such as Roth conversions, tax-efficient investing, and required minimum distributions (RMDs).
    - If you are self-employed or have a unique tax situation, look for a tax advisor who specializes in your specific needs.
- **Fee Structure**:

○ Tax advisors typically charge in a few different ways: hourly rates, flat fees, or a percentage of assets managed. Ensure you understand how the advisor charges and whether the costs align with your budget.

○ For retirement planning, advisors who charge flat fees or hourly rates are often a good option, as they are less likely to have conflicts of interest.

- **Communication Skills**:

○ Tax matters can be complex, so it's essential that the tax advisor can explain concepts clearly and in a way you understand. Good communication ensures that you are informed and empowered to make decisions about your retirement.

- **Trustworthiness**:

○ Look for an advisor who acts in your best interest. This can be verified by checking their disciplinary history (through the **Financial Industry Regulatory Authority (FINRA)** or **State Boards of Accountancy**).

○ You can also ask for references from other clients or check reviews online to get an idea of their reputation.

3. What Services to Expect from a Tax Advisor:

A good tax advisor will offer a range of services tailored to your retirement planning needs:

- **Tax Planning for Retirement Accounts**:

○ They will assess which accounts you should prioritize for contributions. For example, should you invest more in a **401(k)** for tax deferral or a **Roth IRA** for tax-free growth? Understanding how taxes will impact your retirement distributions is essential.

- Tax advisors can also help you understand **required minimum distributions (RMDs)** and how to plan for them in the most tax-efficient manner.

- **Tax-Efficient Withdrawal Strategies**:
  - A tax advisor will help you devise a withdrawal strategy for your retirement accounts that minimizes your tax liability in retirement. This includes deciding whether to draw funds from tax-deferred accounts (like 401(k)s or Traditional IRAs) or tax-free accounts (like Roth IRAs).

- **Social Security Strategy**:
  - They can assist you in planning when to start taking **Social Security benefits** based on your tax situation, as your benefits are subject to income tax.

- **Estate and Inheritance Tax Planning**:
  - If you plan to leave assets to heirs, a tax advisor can help structure your estate to minimize the tax burden on your beneficiaries. This includes setting up trusts, tax-efficient gifting, and managing estate tax implications.

- **Roth Conversions**:
  - Roth conversions can be an effective strategy to reduce future taxes in retirement, especially if you are in a lower tax bracket now than you expect to be in the future. A tax advisor can analyze whether a Roth conversion is beneficial for you based on your income projections and tax situation.

- **Tax Impact of Retirement Plans**:
  - Tax advisors will assess the long-term tax implications of your retirement plan. For example, will the taxes on your retirement savings be manageable based on your future income? Will your tax bracket increase significantly in retirement?

4. How to Shop for the Best Tax Advisor:

1. **Seek Referrals**:

○ Ask friends, family, colleagues, or financial planners for recommendations. Personal referrals are often the best way to find a trustworthy advisor.

○ If you have a specific need, like business ownership or real estate investments, look for a tax advisor who specializes in those areas.

2. **Use Professional Directories**:

○ Websites like **AICPA** (American Institute of Certified Public Accountants), **National Association of Enrolled Agents (NAEA)**, or **CFP Board** can help you find qualified tax professionals near you.

3. **Conduct Interviews**:

○ Before hiring a tax advisor, schedule an initial consultation to discuss your retirement goals, tax situation, and what services the advisor offers. Ask about their experience with retirement planning and tax-efficient strategies.

4. **Check Credentials and Reviews**:

○ Verify the advisor's credentials through their professional organizations (AICPA, NAEA, CFP Board, etc.). You can also look for online reviews and check the advisor's background for any complaints or disciplinary actions.

5. **Understand Fees**:

○ Make sure you understand the fee structure. Ask for an explanation of how the advisor charges and what services are included in the fee. A clear fee structure prevents surprises down the line.

5. Tax Strategies for Retirement Planning:

- **Tax-Deferred Growth**: Contributing to tax-deferred accounts like a **401(k)** or **Traditional IRA** allows your money to grow without being taxed until withdrawal. Your tax advisor can help you determine how much to contribute to these accounts based on your current and expected future tax brackets.
- **Tax-Free Growth**: Contributing to a **Roth IRA** or **Roth 401(k)** allows for tax-free growth and tax-free withdrawals in retirement. Your tax advisor will analyze whether Roth accounts are a good option for you, especially if you're in a lower tax bracket now than you anticipate being in retirement.
- **Tax-Efficient Withdrawals**: In retirement, your advisor will help you create a strategy for withdrawing funds from your retirement accounts in a way that minimizes your tax burden. For example, you may want to draw from tax-deferred accounts first, allowing your Roth IRA to grow tax-free for longer.
- **Utilizing Tax Credits**: There are tax credits available for retirement savings, such as the **Saver's Credit** for low- to moderate-income taxpayers who contribute to retirement plans. A tax advisor will help you identify and claim any credits you're eligible for.
- **Maximizing Employer Contributions**: Ensure that you are taking full advantage of your employer's 401(k) match. A tax advisor can help you determine how much to contribute to your 401(k) to maximize this benefit while minimizing your tax liability.

6. Conclusion:

Choosing a tax advisor for retirement planning is an essential step to ensure that your retirement savings are optimized for tax efficiency. A qualified tax advisor will help you navigate complex tax rules, strategize your retirement withdrawals, and minimize taxes throughout your retirement. To find the best tax advisor, seek referrals, use professional directories, and assess their experience, credentials, and fees. With the right advisor, you can build a tax-efficient retirement plan that ensures you keep more of your money throughout your retirement years.

Chapter 9
Women and Finances

An Overview

Women and finance is a topic that encompasses the financial challenges and opportunities unique to women, as well as strategies to ensure their financial empowerment and independence. Historically, women have faced significant barriers to financial equality, including lower wages, fewer investment opportunities, and limited access to financial education. Despite these obstacles, women have made considerable strides in gaining financial independence and achieving financial goals, both for themselves and their families.

As the financial landscape continues to evolve, it is increasingly important for women to understand and manage their finances, make informed financial decisions, and take active steps toward financial security.

Why Women's Financial Literacy and Independence Matter

There are several reasons why women's engagement with financial matters is critical:

1. Gender Pay Gap

The gender pay gap remains one of the most significant financial challenges that women face. Women, on average, earn less than men for the same work. According to various studies, women earn roughly 80-85 cents for every dollar a man makes. This pay gap can have long-term effects on women's ability to save, invest, and build wealth, leaving them at a financial disadvantage, especially in retirement.

- **Impact**: Lower earnings often translate into lower savings and reduced ability to invest in growth opportunities like real estate, stocks, or retirement accounts. This leaves women more vulnerable to financial insecurity in later years, especially in retirement.

2. Longer Life Expectancy

Women, on average, live longer than men, which means they face a longer retirement period. A longer life expectancy increases the likelihood of needing more financial resources in retirement, especially since women are more likely to live alone as they age.

- **Impact**: Without adequate retirement planning, women are at risk of outliving their savings. A long life expectancy requires proper planning to ensure that women maintain financial independence and do not rely on family members or government support.

3. Role of Caregivers

Women are more likely than men to take on caregiving responsibilities for children, elderly parents, or spouses. This can lead to career interruptions, lower lifetime earnings, and limited ability to save for the future. Many women leave the workforce for extended periods to care for loved ones, which can reduce their lifetime earnings and hinder their ability to save for retirement.

- **Impact**: Career interruptions and reduced income can result in lower retirement savings and a smaller pension, making it more difficult for women to maintain their financial independence as they age.

4. Financial Independence and Empowerment

Financial independence is the ability to manage one's finances, invest wisely, and make decisions without relying on a partner or family member. Financial empowerment for women means having control over their own economic destiny, reducing the risk of financial abuse, and improving self-esteem and confidence.

- **Impact**: Achieving financial independence provides women with more choices, including the ability to leave unhealthy relationships, invest in their education, and pursue opportunities for career advancement. It also leads to a greater sense of security and freedom.

5. Retirement Planning

Women, on average, save less for retirement than men. This is due to a combination of factors, including the gender pay gap, caregiving responsibilities, and longer life expectancy. Many women underestimate how much they will need in retirement and fail to invest sufficiently during their working years.

- **Impact**: A lack of proper retirement savings can lead to financial hardship in retirement, making it crucial for women to start saving early and to invest in long-term strategies like 401(k)s IRAs, or other retirement vehicles.

Key Areas of Focus for Women in Finance

To address the financial disparities that women face and ensure their financial security, several key areas are vital for women to understand and act upon:

1. Financial Education

Knowledge is power when it comes to managing finances. Financial literacy is the foundation of smart financial decision-making, and it empowers women to take control of their financial future. This includes understanding how to budget, save, invest, and protect wealth.

- **Why it's important**: The more informed women are about financial matters, the more likely they are to take proactive steps toward wealth-building and financial independence.

Financial education also helps women make confident decisions about their financial future, whether they are saving for retirement, purchasing a home, or managing debt.

2. Investment Strategies

Women should become comfortable with investing, whether in stocks, bonds, mutual funds, or real estate. Long-term investments can generate wealth, protect against inflation, and help build assets for retirement or other financial goals.

- **Why it's important**: Historically, women have been less likely to invest due to fear, lack of confidence, or societal norms. However, learning about investment strategies, such as diversifying your portfolio or using tax-advantaged accounts like IRAs, can help women increase their wealth and ensure a more comfortable retirement.

3. Debt Management

Debt, particularly student loans, and credit card debt, is a significant barrier to financial freedom for many women. Learning how to manage and eliminate debt is crucial for building wealth and securing financial independence.

- **Why it's important**: Managing debt responsibly and avoiding excessive debt burdens can help women free up money for savings and investment. Reducing debt also improves credit scores, making it easier to access favorable interest rates on loans or mortgages.

4. Building Credit

Credit is an essential tool for financing major life expenses like buying a house, purchasing a car, or even starting a business. Building a strong credit score helps women access better financial products and save money through lower interest rates.

- **Why it's important**: A strong credit history opens doors to opportunities and financial products with favorable terms. Women who understand how to manage credit wisely will be better positioned to make large purchases, secure loans, and grow their wealth.

5. Financial Planning for Life Stages

Women should have a financial plan that aligns with their life stages. This includes planning for major milestones, such as buying a home, marriage, starting a family, or retirement. Having a clear financial plan helps women stay on track and avoid financial setbacks.

- **Why it's important**: Financial planning helps women anticipate future financial needs and make informed decisions along the way. It provides a roadmap for managing resources and preparing for life events such as college expenses, healthcare needs, or home ownership.

Empowering Women Through Financial Independence

The journey toward financial independence requires a proactive approach and a commitment to continuous learning. It's important to recognize that the financial challenges women face are not insurmountable. With the right strategies, tools, and mindset, women can overcome these obstacles and achieve long-term financial success. Here's how to further empower yourself through sound financial decisions:

1. Start Early and Save Consistently

One of the most powerful ways to build wealth is through the principle of compounding—where the money you save grows exponentially over time. The earlier you start saving and investing, the more time your money has to work for you. Even small contributions can grow into large sums over time.

- **Why it's important**: Starting early helps women take advantage of the time factor in growing their wealth, making it easier to weather unexpected financial setbacks. It also provides more opportunities to take risks, which can pay off in the long run.

2. Emergency Fund: A Safety Net for Peace of Mind

An emergency fund is an essential component of any financial plan, as it provides a cushion for unexpected expenses such as medical bills, car repairs, or job loss. Having an emergency fund can prevent you from relying on credit cards or loans in times of crisis.

- **Why it's important**: Building an emergency fund gives women peace of mind, knowing that they are financially prepared for life's uncertainties. This security helps prevent financial stress, allowing you to stay focused on your long-term goals.

3. Be Aware of the Gender Investment Gap

Research shows that women tend to invest less aggressively than men, often opting for safer, lower-yield options. While being conservative can be part of a healthy investment strategy, it's important for women to recognize the potential opportunity in taking calculated risks, particularly when saving for long-term goals like retirement.

- **Why it's important**: Women who invest wisely can see their wealth grow significantly over time, as stocks and equities generally offer higher returns compared to other investment vehicles. Being aware of this investment gap and taking steps to address it can help women build wealth more efficiently.

4. Seek Professional Guidance When Needed

Managing personal finances can be overwhelming, especially when there are numerous investment options, tax laws, and financial products to navigate. A financial advisor or planner can help women make informed decisions about budgeting, retirement planning, investment strategies, and tax planning.

- **Why it's important**: Professional guidance can help ensure that financial decisions align with long-term goals, such as retirement or funding a child's education. Advisors can also offer strategies to minimize tax liabilities and improve overall financial health, which can be especially valuable for women with complex financial situations.

5. Advocating for Equal Pay

As part of the broader conversation around women and finance, advocating for equal pay is essential for ensuring that women have the financial resources they need to thrive. Negotiating for fair wages and equal opportunities in the workplace can have a profound impact on a woman's financial future.

- **Why it's important**: Equal pay not only affects women's immediate income but also influences long-term financial growth by enabling women to save and invest more. It also reduces the pay gap over a woman's lifetime, which can lead to greater financial security and independence.

6. Building a Financial Legacy

Creating a financial legacy for future generations is an important goal for many women. This includes saving for children's education, purchasing a home, and establishing a family business or trust. Women who actively plan for the financial well-being of their families can help build generational wealth and ensure that their loved ones are financially secure.

- **Why it's important**: A financial legacy provides the foundation for future generations to thrive. Women who understand and manage their finances are in a better position to leave a lasting legacy that empowers their families and creates opportunities for their children or grandchildren.

7. Overcoming Financial Fears

Many women experience anxiety or fear when it comes to money—whether it's about not being able to save enough, making poor investment decisions, or facing unforeseen financial hardships. Overcoming these fears requires education, confidence, and a mindset shift toward seeing money as a tool for empowerment rather than stress.

- **Why it's important**: Overcoming financial fears allows women to take control of their finances without being paralyzed by anxiety. Financial confidence leads to better decision-making and the ability to pursue opportunities that might have previously seemed out of reach.

The Future of Women and Finance

The future of women and finance is one of increased financial literacy, empowerment, and opportunity. While women have historically faced challenges related to income inequality and financial management, the growing availability of resources, education, and support systems means that more women are actively taking charge of their financial destinies.

By understanding key financial concepts, prioritizing financial independence, and overcoming barriers such as the gender pay gap, women can build wealth, achieve financial security, and ultimately create lives of freedom and choice. Whether it's through smart investments, debt management, or advocating for equal pay, women who embrace financial literacy will be better positioned to shape their futures and influence the financial systems around them.

Ultimately, financial independence is not just a personal achievement—it's a powerful step toward equality, empowerment, and the ability to live a life on your own terms. Women, now more than ever, have the tools, resources, and knowledge at their disposal to take control of their finances and create a brighter, more secure future for themselves and generations to come.

Conclusion: The Importance of Financial Independence for Women

Achieving financial independence is a critical goal for women, not only for their personal well-being but also for the broader societal impact. Women who are financially independent are better equipped to make choices that align with their personal goals and aspirations. Whether it's securing a comfortable retirement, supporting their families, or pursuing their dreams, understanding and mastering personal finance is a powerful tool for creating a better future.

By breaking down financial barriers, addressing pay equity, prioritizing financial education, and encouraging active investment strategies, women can level the playing field and ensure that they have the financial means to lead fulfilling, independent lives.

9.1 Status of Women in the Management of Personal Finance

Status of Women in the Management of Personal Finance

The role of women in the management of personal finance has evolved significantly over the years. Historically, women were often excluded from financial decision-making, with many relying on their husbands or male family members to handle finances. However, today, women are increasingly taking control of their financial lives, demonstrating greater financial independence, literacy, and confidence. Despite this progress, significant challenges still exist, and understanding the current landscape is crucial to advancing the financial well-being of women.

1. Financial Independence and Empowerment

In recent decades, women have gained access to a wider range of opportunities and resources to manage their personal finances. As more women enter the workforce and attain higher education, they are better equipped to manage their own money, invest, and plan for the future.

- **Workforce Participation**: Women's participation in the workforce has risen significantly, and many women are now breadwinners or co-breadwinners for their families. With increased earning potential, women are able to make more decisions about budgeting, saving, and investing, leading to greater financial independence.

- **Education and Financial Literacy**: Studies show that women are increasingly prioritizing financial literacy. More women are pursuing financial education, attending financial planning workshops, and accessing financial tools and resources online. As a result, they are becoming more confident in managing their finances, from budgeting to investing.

- **Impact of Financial Empowerment**: Financial independence allows women to make decisions based on their desires and needs, rather than being limited by financial constraints. This includes choices about careers, education, health, and retirement. Empowered women are more likely to make strategic financial decisions, take calculated risks, and invest in their future.

2. Challenges Women Face in Personal Finance

Despite progress, there are still several challenges that affect women's financial decision-making and their ability to achieve financial independence.

- **The Gender Pay Gap**: Women continue to earn less than men on average, which limits their ability to save, invest, and accumulate wealth. According to reports, women earn about 82 cents for every dollar earned by men, and this gap is more pronounced for women of color. The pay gap impacts women's financial security, their ability to save for retirement, and their overall wealth-building capacity.

- **Longevity and Retirement Planning**: Women tend to live longer than men, which means they need to plan for a longer retirement. However, due to the gender pay gap, women often have less saved for retirement than men. Additionally, women may face career interruptions for reasons such as caregiving for children or elderly parents, which can result in lower lifetime earnings and fewer retirement savings.

- **Disproportionate Caregiving Roles**: Women are more likely to take on the role of primary caregiver for children, aging parents, or family members with health issues. This can result in career interruptions, reduced earning potential, and a gap in retirement savings. Caregiving responsibilities also make it more difficult for women to focus on long-term financial planning, as short-term expenses and challenges take precedence.

- **Financial Literacy Gaps**: While financial literacy among women is improving, studies indicate that women still lag behind men in certain areas, such as investing and retirement planning. Women are less likely to invest in the stock market and more likely to keep money in low-yield savings accounts. A lack of financial literacy can prevent women from taking full advantage of investment opportunities that could help them build wealth.

3. Women's Strengths in Personal Finance Management

Women often exhibit certain strengths that contribute to effective financial management, and these strengths can be leveraged to improve overall financial outcomes.

- **Risk Aversion and Cautious Investing**: While risk aversion may sometimes hinder women from making aggressive investment moves, it can also be a strength. Women tend to adopt more conservative investment strategies, which can result in more stable long-term wealth accumulation. For example, women are more likely to prioritize savings and ensure that they have an emergency fund.

- **Strong Budgeting Skills**: Many women are adept at budgeting and managing household finances. Women often take a hands-on approach to day-to-day financial management, ensuring that bills are paid on time, expenses are tracked, and savings goals are met. Their attention to detail can help in maintaining financial stability.

- **Long-Term Financial Goals**: Women often focus on long-term financial security, prioritizing savings for future needs such as their children's education or their own retirement. They tend to be more deliberate about saving, and they often set realistic, achievable goals, which can help ensure they stay on track over time.

- **Collaboration in Financial Decision-Making**: Women are more likely than men to seek advice and collaborate on financial decisions. This may involve seeking professional financial advice, talking to family members, or discussing financial matters with a partner. Collaboration often results in more informed and balanced financial decisions.

4. The Role of Financial Education and Resources

Increasing access to financial education and resources is crucial to further empowering women in the management of personal finance.

- **Online Financial Tools**: The growth of digital financial tools, apps, and online platforms has provided women with more accessible and affordable options to manage their finances. Budgeting tools, investment apps, and financial planning websites allow women to take control of their finances and make informed decisions.

- **Financial Coaching and Mentorship**: More women are seeking the guidance of financial coaches and mentors, who can provide advice tailored to their specific financial needs. Financial coaching helps women navigate challenges such as debt management, retirement planning, and investing. Peer mentoring programs have also become popular, allowing women to share their experiences and learn from one another.

- **Workplace Financial Benefits**: Some employers offer resources to help women with financial planning, such as retirement savings options, financial counseling, and wellness programs. These benefits are especially helpful for women who may face unique financial challenges.

5. Looking Ahead: The Future of Women in Personal Finance

As women continue to embrace financial empowerment, it's essential to further support their journey toward financial equality and independence.

- **Advocating for Equal Pay**: One of the most significant ways to improve women's financial status is to address the gender pay gap. Equal pay for equal work would allow women to build wealth more effectively, save for retirement, and achieve greater financial security.
- **Breaking Down Stereotypes**: Women often face societal expectations about their roles in managing money, but these stereotypes need to be challenged. Women must be empowered to take on roles as investors, entrepreneurs, and leaders in financial decision-making.
- **Promoting Financial Literacy**: Continued efforts to promote financial literacy, particularly in areas like investing, credit management, and retirement planning, can ensure that women have the knowledge they need to make sound financial decisions. Financial literacy programs targeted at women, particularly those in underserved communities, will further narrow the financial literacy gap.

An Exploration of Financial Challenges Women Face and How to Overcome Them

Financial challenges for women are multifaceted and shaped by a variety of factors, including societal expectations, gender inequalities, career interruptions, and differences in financial literacy. Despite significant progress in many areas, women still face unique obstacles when it comes to achieving financial independence and security. However, with increased awareness, financial education, and strategic planning, many of these challenges can be overcome. This exploration identifies key financial challenges women face and offers practical solutions for overcoming them.

1. The Gender Pay Gap

Challenge:

One of the most significant financial challenges women face is the gender pay gap. Women, on average, earn less than men, which can have a cumulative impact on long-term wealth accumulation. According to reports from the U.S. Census Bureau, women earn approximately 82 cents for every dollar earned by men. This pay disparity is even more pronounced for women of color, with Black and Hispanic women earning significantly less than their White counterparts.

The gender pay gap impacts women's ability to save for retirement, invest, and meet long-term financial goals. Lower wages often translate into smaller contributions to savings accounts and a reduced ability to invest in wealth-building opportunities.

Solution:

- **Advocacy for Equal Pay**: One of the most effective long-term solutions is advocacy for equal pay. Women should feel empowered to negotiate salaries and benefits and advocate for equal pay in the workplace. Joining or supporting organizations that promote equal pay can also contribute to systemic change.

- **Leverage Additional Income Streams**: Women can supplement their income by pursuing side hustles, freelance work, or entrepreneurial ventures. Starting a side business or engaging in gig work can help increase financial security and provide more opportunities for saving and investing.

- **Salary Transparency**: Asking about salary ranges upfront when applying for jobs can help ensure that compensation is in line with market rates. Researching salary data from reliable sources such as Glassdoor or the Bureau of Labor Statistics can give women the confidence to negotiate for better pay.

2. Career Interruptions and Caregiving Responsibilities

Challenge:

Women are more likely than men to take career breaks or reduce their work hours due to caregiving responsibilities. This includes taking time off to care for children, elderly parents, or family members with health issues. These career interruptions can lead to reduced earning potential, fewer retirement savings, and missed opportunities for career advancement.

Solution:

- **Plan for Career Interruptions**: Women can anticipate potential caregiving roles by creating flexible career plans. This might include maintaining a strong professional network, taking on part-time or remote work opportunities, or negotiating flexible work arrangements that allow them to balance caregiving responsibilities with their career.
- **Utilize Family Leave Benefits**: Many countries and employers offer paid family leave or parental leave, which can help mitigate the financial impact of taking time off for caregiving. Women should take advantage of these benefits when possible.
- **Build an Emergency Fund**: Having an emergency savings fund can provide financial stability during times of caregiving. An emergency fund acts as a buffer that can cover living expenses when a woman has to take time off from work to care for a family member.
- **Consider Long-Term Care Insurance**: As the caregiving role often involves looking after elderly parents, it's worth considering long-term care insurance. This can ease the financial burden if the need for caregiving arises later in life.

3. Lower Retirement Savings

Challenge:

Women tend to have lower retirement savings than men, largely due to the gender pay gap, career interruptions, and longer life expectancy. Women are also more likely to live in poverty in their later years, particularly if they are widowed, divorced, or have limited savings. A lack of adequate retirement planning can leave women financially vulnerable in their golden years.

Solution:

- **Start Saving Early**: It's essential for women to start saving for retirement as early as possible, even if it's just a small amount. The earlier they start, the more they can benefit from compound interest. Setting up automatic contributions to retirement accounts, such as a 401(k) or an IRA, ensures consistent savings.
- **Maximize Employer Retirement Contributions**: If available, women should take full advantage of employer-sponsored retirement plans, especially if the employer offers matching contributions. It's essentially "free money" that can significantly boost retirement savings.
- **Consider Catch-Up Contributions**: Women aged 50 and above can make catch-up contributions to their retirement accounts, allowing them to save more money in their later years. These additional contributions can be particularly useful for women who may not have saved as much earlier in life.
- **Diversify Investments**: Women should also ensure their retirement portfolios are diversified across different asset classes to maximize growth potential. Consulting with a financial planner can help ensure the portfolio aligns with their long-term retirement goals.

4. Financial Literacy Gaps

Challenge:

Despite improvements in financial literacy, studies show that women still lag behind men in areas such as investing, credit management, and retirement planning. Women may also be less likely to take risks with their money, often opting for low-risk, low-return investments that don't grow their wealth as quickly as other options.

Solution:

- **Invest in Financial Education**: Women can overcome financial literacy gaps by investing time and effort into learning about personal finance. Reading books, attending workshops, or using online resources such as blogs, podcasts, or videos can improve their understanding of budgeting, investing, taxes, and debt management.

- **Engage a Financial Advisor**: Consulting with a certified financial planner or advisor can help women navigate complex financial decisions. A financial advisor can provide personalized advice on how to maximize investments, save for retirement, and avoid financial pitfalls.

- **Invest for the Future**: Women should consider diversifying their investments, including stocks, bonds, mutual funds, and real estate. While women are generally more risk-averse than men, taking calculated risks can help generate long-term wealth.

5. Social and Cultural Barriers

Challenge:

Cultural norms and societal expectations often play a role in how women approach money and finance. Women have historically been expected to prioritize family and household duties over personal financial growth. Additionally, there are social stigmas surrounding women and money, which may discourage women from taking charge of their financial futures.

Solution:

- **Challenge Gender Norms**: Women can take the initiative to challenge traditional gender norms related to money and finances. This might involve seeking education on investment, learning how to manage money in a marriage or partnership, and setting financial goals independent of societal expectations.

- **Encourage Financial Conversations**: Women should start conversations about finances with their partners, peers, and mentors. Sharing financial knowledge and experiences helps create a supportive network and removes the taboo surrounding women and money.

- **Financial Empowerment**: Embrace financial empowerment by taking small, consistent steps toward achieving financial goals. This includes creating a budget, building an emergency fund, and making intentional savings and investment choices.

Conclusion

While women face unique financial challenges, these obstacles are not insurmountable. By understanding the barriers they face—whether it be pay inequality, caregiving responsibilities, or financial illiteracy—women can take proactive steps to overcome them. Through strategic planning, continuous education, and leveraging available resources, women can achieve financial independence, secure their futures, and break the cycle of financial dependence. The key is to recognize the challenges, take control, and adopt a mindset of financial empowerment that will lead to long-term success.

9.4 Estate Planning

Why estate planning is crucial for women and how to create a will, set up trusts, and plan for financial security.

Why Estate Planning is Crucial for Women and How to Create a Will, Set Up Trusts, and Plan for Financial Security

Estate planning is a critical aspect of financial security that is often overlooked, especially by women. Many women underestimate the importance of planning for their future, leaving their assets and wishes unprotected. Whether single, married, or a mother, estate planning ensures that women have control over how their wealth is distributed, how their healthcare will be managed, and how their loved ones will be taken care of after they are gone. Without proper estate planning, women risk leaving their families in confusion, facing unnecessary taxes, and potentially complicating the management of their affairs.

In this section, we'll explain why estate planning is particularly crucial for women and offer guidance on how to create a will, set up trusts, and plan for financial security.

Why Estate Planning is Crucial for Women

1. **Longer Life Expectancy**: Women generally live longer than men, which means they are more likely to face health complications as they age. Estate planning ensures that their assets are protected and that they are not a burden on their family members in the later years. It also allows women to plan for long-term care needs and ensure their financial stability throughout retirement.

2. **Wealth Transfer**: Women are often the primary caretakers of their families, and as such, they may accumulate substantial wealth over their lifetime. Proper estate planning helps ensure that wealth is transferred efficiently and in line with their wishes. Without a clear plan, the distribution of assets could result in unnecessary probate fees, family disputes, or unintended beneficiaries.

3. **Single or Divorced Women**: Women who are single or divorced face unique estate planning challenges. Without a spouse to assume financial responsibility, women need to ensure they have clear plans in place for how their assets will be managed and passed on. Additionally, many single women neglect to name a trusted individual to make medical and financial decisions on their behalf in the event of incapacity.

4. **Caregiving and Guardianship**: Women are more likely to be the primary caregivers for children or elderly parents. Estate planning allows them to designate guardians for minor children and make provisions for loved ones who may need long-term care. This can provide peace of mind knowing that their loved ones will be taken care of according to their wishes, especially in the event of an unexpected illness or death.

5. **Tax Planning**: Estate planning helps minimize estate taxes and maximize the wealth passed on to heirs. Women who have significant assets may want to avoid excessive taxes through strategies such as gifting, charitable donations, and using tax-efficient trusts.

Key Components of Estate Planning for Women

1. **Creating a Will**: A will is a legal document that outlines how a person's assets should be distributed after death. For women, creating a will is the most essential part of estate planning. Without a will, the state will decide how to distribute your assets, which may not align with your wishes. Here's how to create a will:

   - **List Your Assets**: Start by identifying all your assets, including real estate, bank accounts, retirement funds, personal belongings, and business interests.
   - **Choose Beneficiaries**: Decide who will inherit your assets. This could include family members, friends, or charities.
   - **Name an Executor**: Choose someone you trust to manage the distribution of your assets and ensure that your wishes are carried out.
   - **Select a Guardian for Minor Children**: If you have children, you need to name a legal guardian to care for them if both you and your partner pass away.
   - **Review and Update Regularly**: As your circumstances change (e.g., marriage, divorce, the birth of children), review and update your will to ensure it reflects your current wishes.

2. **Setting Up Trusts**: A trust is a legal arrangement where a person (the "trustee") holds and manages assets on behalf of another person (the "beneficiary"). Trusts are particularly useful for women who want to ensure their assets are protected, provide for loved ones, or minimize estate taxes. There are several types of trusts:

- **Revocable Living Trust**: This trust allows you to retain control over your assets while you're alive and makes it easy to update or revoke them if necessary. After your death, the assets in the trust are distributed according to your wishes without going through probate.
- **Irrevocable Trust**: Once established, you cannot change the terms or take assets back. This type of trust can help reduce estate taxes and protect assets from creditors.
- **Testamentary Trust**: This trust is created within your will and comes into effect only after your death. It is commonly used to provide for minor children or family members who need ongoing financial management.
- **Charitable Trust**: A charitable remainder trust (CRT) allows you to donate assets to a charity while retaining income from the assets during your lifetime. It can reduce estate taxes and provide tax deductions.

Trusts can be a vital tool for protecting wealth and ensuring it is used according to your wishes.

3. **Designating Powers of Attorney**: In estate planning, it is critical to appoint someone to make decisions on your behalf if you are unable to do so. Powers of attorney come in two forms:

- **Financial Power of Attorney**: This person is authorized to manage your financial affairs if you become incapacitated. This includes paying bills, managing investments, and filing taxes.
- **Healthcare Power of Attorney**: This person is authorized to make medical decisions for you if you cannot communicate your wishes. This includes decisions about medical treatments, life support, and end-of-life care.

4. **Planning for Health Care and Long-Term Care**: As women age, they may face health-related challenges that require long-term care. It's important to plan for how healthcare will be managed:

- **Living Will**: A living will outline your preferences for medical treatment in the event that you are unable to communicate them, especially if you are in a terminal condition or unable to make decisions.

- **Long-Term Care Insurance**: This insurance helps cover the costs of long-term care services, such as nursing home care or in-home care, which can be particularly important for women as they live longer.

5. **Minimizing Estate Taxes**: Estate taxes can significantly reduce the amount of wealth passed on to heirs. By using strategies like gifting assets during your lifetime, establishing trusts, and taking advantage of tax-free gift allowances, you can reduce the tax burden on your estate.

Steps for Creating a Comprehensive Estate Plan

1. **Assess Your Financial Situation**: Before creating a will or trust, assess your assets, debts, and financial situation. This will help you determine how to divide your estate and what provisions need to be made for your family members.

2. **Consult with an Estate Planning Attorney**: Estate planning laws can be complex, so it's wise to consult with an attorney who specializes in this area. They can help ensure that your documents are legally sound and aligned with your goals.

3. **Choose Trusted Executors, Trustees, and Beneficiaries**: Select individuals who you trust to manage your estate according to your wishes. This includes choosing an executor for your will, trustees for any trusts, and beneficiaries for your assets.

4. **Update Your Plan as Life Changes**: Regularly review and update your estate plan as your life circumstances change (e.g., marriage, divorce, the birth of children, or changes in financial status). This will ensure your estate plan remains relevant and effective.

Estate planning is an essential part of securing financial stability and ensuring that your wishes are respected after your death. For women, it provides the tools necessary to protect their assets, minimize taxes, and secure the future of their loved ones. By creating a will, setting up trusts, and planning for financial and healthcare needs, women can ensure their financial legacy is protected and that they are ready for the unexpected.

Conclusion

The status of women in the management of personal finance is rapidly improving, but there is still work to be done. Women today are more financially empowered than ever before, but challenges like the gender pay gap, caregiving responsibilities, and lower financial literacy still create barriers to financial independence. By continuing to prioritize financial education, closing the wage gap, and promoting women's leadership in financial decision-making, we can pave the way for a more financially secure future for women everywhere. With the right tools, resources, and mindset, women can achieve financial freedom and create a legacy of financial empowerment for future generations.

An exploration of financial challenges women face and how to overcome them

Certainly! Here's the updated message with the nationwide service information included before the firm details:

Nationwide Service Availability of Tax Advisors for Women

Many of the financial advisory firms listed below offer nationwide services, though their offices or primary locations may be in specific areas. The firms that operate on a national scale often have virtual capabilities, enabling them to serve clients no matter their geographic location. Here's a summary of each firm's service availability:

1. Mission Wealth

- **Nationwide Services**: Yes, they serve clients nationwide, though they have offices in various locations.

2. Ellevest

- **Nationwide Services**: Yes, Ellevest is an online platform, so their services are available nationwide.

3. Mercer Advisors

- **Nationwide Services**: Yes, Mercer Advisors has offices across the United States and provides services nationwide.

4. Blue Mountain Financial Planning, LLC

- **Nationwide Services**: This firm is based in Melissa, TX, but it provides services to clients nationwide, primarily through virtual meetings.

5. Waverly Advisors

- **Nationwide Services**: Yes, Waverly Advisors has multiple offices and provides services nationwide.

6. Forbes' Top Women Wealth Advisors

- **Nationwide Services**: Yes, this list includes advisors from across the U.S. You can filter for advisors in your specific location or region.

7. Investopedia Advisor Council

- **Nationwide Services**: Yes, the advisors on this council are based across the U.S., and their resources can be accessed by clients nationwide.

8. Cornerstone Wealth Group

- **Nationwide Services**: Yes, Cornerstone Wealth Group provides services to clients across the U.S., though they have offices in specific regions.

9. Retirement Tax Services

- **Nationwide Services**: Yes, they offer services nationwide, as their focus is on providing tax planning services remotely in collaboration with financial advisors.

10. Best Path Advisors

- **Nationwide Services**: Yes, Best Path Advisors serve clients across the U.S., although they have offices in specific locations.

1. Mission Wealth

Mission Wealth offers financial planning services tailored for women, recognizing the unique challenges they face. Their female financial advisors specialize in retirement planning, estate and trust management, investment strategies, and tax management. They aim to help women create comprehensive financial plans that provide for their futures.

- **Website**: Mission Wealth
- **Services**: Financial planning, retirement planning, investment strategies, tax management
- **Location**: Multiple locations; services available nationwide
- **Source**: Mission Wealth

2. Ellevest

Ellevest is a financial advisory firm focused on women's wealth and financial guidance. They offer financial planning, online investing, private wealth management, retirement planning, and more, all tailored to women's specific financial needs.

- **Website**: Ellevest
- **Services**: Financial planning, investing, retirement planning, wealth management
- **Location**: Online services available nationwide
- **Source**: Ellevest

3. Mercer Advisors

Mercer Advisors provides comprehensive financial planning services with a focus on women's wealth. They offer financial planning, investment management, tax planning, estate planning, and retirement planning, all designed to address the unique financial challenges women face.

- **Website**: Mercer Advisors
- **Services**: Financial planning, investment management, tax planning, estate planning, retirement planning
- **Location**: Offices across the U.S.; services available nationwide
- **Source**: Mercer Advisors

4. Blue Mountain Financial Planning, LLC

Based in Melissa, TX, Blue Mountain Financial Planning, led by Hannah Szarszewski, CFP®, AFC®, offers comprehensive financial planning services with a focus on integrating financial coaching and education. They cater to clients of all ages, helping them achieve financial independence and live life to the fullest.

- **Website**: Blue Mountain Financial Planning

- **Services**: Comprehensive financial planning, retirement planning, investment management, tax planning
- **Location**: Melissa, TX
- **Source**: Blue Mountain Financial Planning

5. Waverly Advisors

Waverly Advisors offers a specialized service called Waverly Women, led by female advisors. This service combines expertise in financial, investment, tax, and estate planning to address the unique needs of women.

- **Website**: Waverly Advisors
- **Services**: Comprehensive financial planning, investment management, tax planning, estate planning
- **Location**: Offices in multiple locations; services available nationwide
- **Source**: Waverly Advisors

6. Forbes' Top Women Wealth Advisors

Forbes publishes an annual list of America's Top Women Advisors, highlighting leading female financial advisors across the country. This list can serve as a valuable resource for identifying reputable advisors who specialize in serving women's financial needs.

- **Website**: Forbes' Top Women Wealth Advisors
- **Services**: Varies by advisor; includes retirement planning, investment management, tax planning, and more
- **Location**: Nationwide
- **Source**: Forbes

7. Investopedia Advisor Council

The Investopedia Advisor Council comprises a group of independent U.S.-based financial advisors, including those who focus on serving women. Members share their expertise through articles, webinars, and other educational initiatives, aiming to empower individuals with financial literacy and education.

- **Website**: Investopedia Advisor Council
- **Services**: Financial education, articles, webinars, and resources
- **Location**: Advisors are based nationwide
- **Source**: Investopedia

8. Cornerstone Wealth Group

Cornerstone Wealth Group offers tax planning services as part of their comprehensive financial planning. They work with clients annually to review financial situations, optimize tax outcomes, and adapt to changes in tax laws and personal circumstances.

- **Website**: Cornerstone Wealth Group
- **Services**: Tax planning, retirement planning, investment management
- **Location**: Multiple locations; services available nationwide
- **Source**: Cornerstone Wealth Group

9. Retirement Tax Services

Retirement Tax Services partners with financial advisors to deliver tax planning strategies, helping clients optimize tax outcomes and minimize liabilities, especially during retirement.

- **Website**: Retirement Tax Services
- **Services**: Tax planning, retirement tax strategies

- **Location**: Services available nationwide
- **Source**: Retirement Tax Services

10. Best Path Advisors

Best Path Advisors specializes in retirement planning, tax planning, wealth management, and risk management for women and couples over age 50. They offer personalized strategies to maximize income, minimize taxes, and grow and preserve wealth.

- **Website**: Best Path Advisors
- **Services**: Retirement planning, tax planning, wealth management, risk management
- **Location**: Multiple locations; services available nationwide
- **Source**: Best Path Advisors

When selecting a tax advisor, consider factors such as credentials (e.g., Certified Financial Planner [CFP®], Certified Public Accountant [CPA]), experience in serving women's financial needs, fee structures, and client reviews. It's advisable to consult with multiple advisors to find one whose services align with your specific financial goals and needs.

Chapter 10
Insurance

Understanding Insurance and Its Importance

Insurance is a financial arrangement designed to protect individuals, businesses, and assets against potential risks and unforeseen events. It operates on the principle of risk management, where policyholders pay premiums to an insurance provider in exchange for financial protection against specific losses. These losses may stem from health issues, accidents, property damage, liability claims, or even life events.

Insurance plays a crucial role in achieving financial freedom, as it serves as a safeguard against financial setbacks that could derail long-term wealth-building efforts. Without insurance, an unexpected event—such as a medical emergency, car accident, or natural disaster—could lead to devastating financial consequences, forcing individuals to deplete their savings or fall into debt.

There are various types of insurance, each serving a unique purpose in securing financial stability:

- Health Insurance: Covers medical expenses, reducing the burden of high healthcare costs.
- Life Insurance: Provides financial security to loved ones in case of the policyholder's passing.
- Auto Insurance: Protects against damages, theft, or liabilities related to vehicles.

- Homeowners/Renters Insurance: Safeguards property and personal belongings from unforeseen damages or theft.
- Disability Insurance: Offers income protection in case of illness or injury that prevents one from working.
- Business Insurance: Shields enterprises from financial risks, liability claims, and operational disruptions.

In the pursuit of financial freedom, insurance acts as a financial safety net that prevents setbacks from turning into long-term financial struggles. By integrating proper insurance planning into financial strategies, individuals and families can protect their wealth, ensure stability, and focus on wealth-building without fear of catastrophic financial loss.

As emphasized in *Unleashing Financial Freedom*, true financial independence is not just about increasing income and investments—it's also about mitigating risks that threaten financial security. A well-structured insurance plan is an essential component of financial planning, ensuring that unforeseen circumstances do not derail the journey to financial empowerment.

By understanding the significance of insurance and choosing the right policies, individuals can take proactive steps toward protecting their financial future, securing their assets, and ultimately achieving lasting financial freedom.

Unleashing Financial Freedom Through Proper Insurance Planning

Financial freedom is a goal that many individuals and families aspire to achieve. It represents a state where financial security, stability, and growth are no longer concerns but rather components of a well-structured financial strategy. One critical yet often overlooked aspect of achieving financial freedom is integrating proper insurance planning into one's financial framework. By ensuring that assets, income, and loved ones are adequately protected, individuals can focus on wealth-building without the looming fear of catastrophic financial loss. This document explores how insurance planning contributes to financial freedom, the various types of insurance essential for stability, and strategies to integrate insurance into a holistic financial plan.

The Role of Insurance in Financial Freedom

Insurance serves as a safeguard against unforeseen financial setbacks. Without it, a single event—such as a medical emergency, natural disaster, or unexpected death—can derail years of financial progress. Proper insurance planning ensures that individuals and families are prepared for the unexpected, allowing them to continue their financial journey with confidence. It provides peace of mind and stability, making it a fundamental component of financial independence.

A comprehensive insurance plan does not merely protect against loss; it enhances financial growth by mitigating risks. When an individual knows that their income, health, and assets are protected, they can make bolder financial decisions, invest more aggressively, and focus on long-term wealth accumulation. Without insurance, financial freedom remains fragile and uncertain, as a single misfortune can lead to financial ruin.

Types of Insurance Essential for Financial Stability

To achieve financial freedom, individuals must consider several key types of insurance:

1. **Life Insurance** Life insurance provides financial security for dependents in the event of an untimely death. Whether through term life or whole life insurance, this coverage ensures that loved ones are not burdened with debts, funeral expenses, or a sudden loss of income. It allows families to maintain their standard of living and continue pursuing financial goals.

2. **Health Insurance** Medical expenses are one of the leading causes of financial hardship. A robust health insurance plan covers routine medical costs, emergency care, and long-term treatments, preventing unexpected healthcare expenses from draining savings and investments.

Having adequate health coverage ensures that medical emergencies do not compromise financial stability.

3. **Disability Insurance** The ability to earn an income is one of the most valuable assets an individual possesses. Disability insurance provides financial support in the event of an illness or injury that prevents a person from working. By replacing lost income, this type of insurance ensures that financial obligations continue to be met even when one is unable to work.

4. **Property and Homeowners Insurance** A home is often the most significant investment for many individuals. Homeowners and property insurance protect against damage, theft, and liability risks. In the event of a disaster, such insurance ensures that individuals are not left financially devastated and can rebuild their lives without depleting their savings.

5. **Auto Insurance** Automobile insurance is essential for protecting against financial losses due to accidents, theft, or liability claims. It ensures that damages are covered and that legal or medical expenses do not disrupt financial progress.

6. **Long-Term Care Insurance** As individuals age, the need for long-term care becomes more probable. Whether it is nursing home care, assisted living, or in-home care, long-term care insurance helps protect assets from being eroded by these expenses, preserving wealth for future generations.

7. **Umbrella Insurance** Umbrella insurance provides additional liability coverage above and beyond the limits of your home or auto insurance policies. It is particularly useful if you have significant assets or engage in high-risk activities. Umbrella insurance can protect you from lawsuits and help preserve your wealth in case of legal claims.

Creating a Well-Structured Insurance Plan

To build a comprehensive insurance plan, start by evaluating your personal and financial situation. Consider the following steps:

1. **Assess Your Risks and Needs:** Start by assessing the risks you face based on your lifestyle, health, income, and assets. Consider whether you have dependents who rely on your income or a mortgage that could leave your family financially vulnerable if you were to pass away. Evaluate your health risks and whether you need additional medical coverage, and consider the risks of disability or accidents that could prevent you from working.

2. **Evaluate Coverage Gaps:** Once you identify your needs, review your current insurance coverage and determine if there are any gaps. For example, you might have life insurance but lack disability insurance. Or, your health insurance might not cover specific medical needs. Address these gaps by adding policies that offer the coverage you need.

3. **Consider Your Budget:** Insurance is an ongoing expense, so it's important to balance adequate coverage with your ability to pay premiums. Some types of insurance, like health or life insurance, can be expensive, so it may be necessary to adjust your coverage over time as your financial situation changes. Shop around for policies to find the best value.

4. **Work with Professionals:** To ensure that your insurance plan is comprehensive and aligned with your financial goals, work with professionals who specialize in insurance and financial planning. A certified financial planner (CFP) can help you integrate insurance into your overall financial plan, considering factors like retirement savings, investments, and tax strategies. An insurance agent or broker can help you navigate the wide array of insurance products available, ensuring that you choose policies that are suitable for your needs and budget. They can also provide guidance on policy riders or add-ons that can enhance coverage.

Whom to Consult for Guidance

1. **Certified Financial Planner (CFP):** A CFP is trained to provide advice on all aspects of financial planning, including insurance. They can help you evaluate your needs and ensure that your insurance coverage fits into your larger financial strategy. By working with a CFP, you gain a holistic approach to planning for your future.

2. **Insurance Agent or Broker:** Insurance agents are licensed professionals who can provide guidance on the best insurance products for your specific needs. They work directly with insurance providers and can compare policies to ensure you get the right coverage. Brokers represent multiple insurance companies and can offer unbiased advice on policies.

3. **Tax Advisor:** A tax advisor can help you understand the tax implications of different insurance policies. For example, life insurance policies can offer tax-deferred growth, and contributions to certain health insurance plans may be deductible. Understanding these aspects can help you make more informed decisions and maximize tax benefits.

4. **Estate Planner:** An estate planner can assist in incorporating life insurance and other policies into your estate plan, ensuring that your assets are distributed according to your wishes and minimizing potential estate taxes. They can help you set up trusts or beneficiaries, and guide you on the use of insurance to protect your legacy.

Integrating Insurance into a Financial Strategy

To maximize financial freedom, individuals should incorporate insurance as a key component of their overall financial plan. Here are some strategies for doing so:

1. **Assess Personal Financial Risks** The first step in integrating insurance into a financial strategy is identifying potential risks. Individuals should evaluate their health, lifestyle, employment stability, and asset portfolio to determine what types of insurance coverage are necessary.

2. **Align Insurance with Financial Goals** Insurance policies should complement an individual's broader financial objectives. For example, a person focused on early retirement may require a combination of life, disability, and long-term care insurance to protect their assets and income streams.

3. **Review and Update Policies Regularly** Life circumstances change over time, affecting financial needs. Marriage, children, career advancements, and new investments all require periodic reassessment of insurance policies to ensure adequate coverage.

4. **Optimize Costs without Sacrificing Coverage** While insurance is essential, overpaying for unnecessary coverage can hinder wealth accumulation. Working with financial professionals to balance affordability and protection ensures efficient resource allocation.

5. **Utilize Tax-Advantaged Insurance Options** Some insurance products, such as permanent life insurance and annuities, offer tax-deferred growth, providing additional benefits beyond protection. Leveraging these options strategically can enhance overall financial efficiency.

Conclusion

A well-structured insurance plan is essential for financial security. It acts as a safeguard, ensuring that unforeseen events, such as illness, accidents, or death, do not derail your financial goals. By evaluating your risks, needs, and financial situation, and working with qualified professionals, you can create a plan that provides comprehensive coverage while supporting your broader financial objectives. Properly integrated into your overall financial strategy, insurance allows you to achieve lasting financial empowerment with confidence and security.

Proper insurance planning is an integral part of achieving and maintaining financial freedom. It acts as a protective shield that prevents unexpected events from undermining financial stability. By carefully selecting and integrating the right types of insurance into their financial strategies, individuals and families can safeguard their wealth, ensure long-term stability, and confidently pursue their financial aspirations. With the right insurance in place, financial freedom becomes not just an aspiration but a sustainable reality.

Determining how much insurance coverage is enough for each of the policies mentioned depends on various factors, including your income, lifestyle, dependents, assets, debts, and future goals. Below are some general guidelines and considerations to help you determine the right amount of coverage for each insurance type:

1. Health Insurance

How Much is Enough? The amount of health insurance coverage you need depends on several factors:

- **Healthcare Needs:** Consider your current health, any chronic conditions, and the level of care you may need in the future. If you or your family members have ongoing medical treatments, ensure the policy covers these needs adequately.
- **Premiums and Deductibles:** Look for a balance between the monthly premium you can afford and the deductible (the amount you pay before insurance kicks in). A lower premium often means a higher deductible, and vice versa.
- **Out-of-Pocket Maximum:** Ensure the insurance has a reasonable out-of-pocket maximum that limits how much you will pay for medical services in a year. Ideally, the out-of-pocket maximum should be a figure you could manage in the event of a major illness or accident.

A common rule of thumb is to ensure the health plan provides full coverage for routine medical expenses and emergencies, including hospitalization, prescriptions, and preventive care, and that the out-of-pocket costs are within your budget.

2. Life Insurance

How Much is Enough? The amount of life insurance you need largely depends on your family's financial situation and future goals. Common methods for calculating the right amount of coverage include:

- **The Income Replacement Method:** A popular approach is to buy life insurance that replaces 5-10 times your annual income. This ensures your family can maintain their lifestyle and cover expenses without your income.
- **The Needs-Based Method:** This approach calculates the amount of life insurance needed by assessing your family's expenses, such as:
    - Outstanding debts (mortgage, loans)
    - Future education costs for children
    - Ongoing living expenses
    - Funeral expenses
    - Inflation adjustments

As a simple guideline, many financial experts suggest 10-12 times your annual income, especially if you have dependents who rely on your income.

3. Disability Insurance

How Much is Enough? Disability insurance should replace a significant portion of your income in the event that you are unable to work due to illness or injury. Most disability policies cover between 60% to 70% of your pre-tax income.

Consider these factors when determining coverage:

- **Income Replacement:** Ensure the policy provides enough to cover your regular living expenses and obligations.

- **Benefit Period:** Look for policies that provide long-term coverage (e.g., until you can return to work or reach retirement age).
- **Elimination Period:** The waiting period before benefits start. You can choose a shorter elimination period for faster payout, but this may increase premiums.

For most people, 60-70% of their monthly income is enough to cover essential living expenses, though you may need more if you have significant financial responsibilities, like a mortgage or dependent children.

4. Homeowners or Renters Insurance

How Much is Enough? The amount of homeowners or renter's insurance you need depends on the value of your home and belongings, and your ability to replace them in the event of a disaster.

- **Homeowners Insurance:**
  - **Dwelling Coverage:** Ensure it covers the cost to rebuild your home in the event of a total loss. This should be based on the replacement cost, not the market value, which accounts for land value and current market trends.
  - **Personal Property Coverage:** Coverage should be enough to replace your personal belongings, such as furniture, electronics, and clothing. This amount varies, but you should take inventory of your belongings and estimate their replacement value.
  - **Liability Coverage:** Homeowners insurance typically includes liability coverage, which protects against legal claims for injuries or damages occurring on your property. A common amount of liability coverage is \$300,000 to \$500,000, but you can increase this based on your risk and assets.

- **Renters Insurance:** Renters insurance is typically less expensive than homeowner's insurance, and it covers personal belongings, liability, and temporary living expenses. Ensure the policy covers the value of your possessions and provides enough liability coverage (typically between $100,000 to $300,000).

5. Auto Insurance

How Much is Enough? Auto insurance is required by law, and the amount of coverage you need depends on your state's minimum requirements and your personal financial situation.

- **Liability Coverage:**
  - **Bodily Injury Liability:** This covers injuries to others in an accident you cause. A common recommendation is $100,000 per person and $300,000 per accident.
  - **Property Damage Liability:** This covers damage to other vehicles or property in an accident you cause. A minimum of $50,000 is often recommended.
- **Collision and Comprehensive Coverage:** These cover damages to your own car, regardless of fault, and cover non-collision incidents (e.g., theft, vandalism, natural disasters). Consider this coverage if you have a newer or more valuable car, or if you would struggle to pay for repairs or replacement out-of-pocket.
- **Uninsured/Underinsured Motorist Coverage:** This covers you in case of an accident with someone who doesn't have adequate insurance. This is particularly important if you live in an area with high numbers of uninsured drivers.

A general rule is to have coverage that exceeds the state's minimum requirements and provides enough liability protection in the event of a severe accident.

6. Umbrella Insurance

How Much is Enough? Umbrella insurance offers an extra layer of liability protection, typically in increments of $1 million. The right amount depends on your net worth, lifestyle, and the risks you face.

- **Consider your assets:** If you have significant assets, such as real estate, investments, or savings, umbrella insurance can help protect those assets in the event of a lawsuit. A typical starting point is $1 million of umbrella coverage, but you may need more if you have substantial assets or engage in higher-risk activities (e.g., owning rental properties, having a business, or engaging in activities that could lead to lawsuits).
- **Consider your potential liabilities:** Think about your exposure to lawsuits—do you host parties, drive a lot, or engage in activities that could result in accidents?

Generally, many individuals choose a $1 million umbrella policy, but high-net-worth individuals may need $2 million or more to ensure adequate protection.

General Guidelines for All Types of Insurance:

- **Reevaluate Annually:** Your insurance needs change over time. Annual reviews ensure that your coverage reflects changes in income, assets, dependents, and other life circumstances.
- **Use an Insurance Calculator:** Some online tools help estimate the amount of coverage you may need, based on your personal situation and financial goals.
- **Consult Professionals:** A financial advisor, insurance agent, or broker can help you assess the right amount of coverage based on your unique needs and financial goals.

Conclusion

Determining how much insurance is enough depending on evaluating your financial needs, risks, and goals. While there is no one-size-fits-all answer, the key is ensuring that you are sufficiently covered to protect your family, assets, and future financial plans. Work with qualified professionals to create a tailored insurance strategy that provides comprehensive protection without overspending. By doing so, you ensure that your financial journey is secure, even in the face of life's unexpected events.

7. Long-Term Care Insurance

How Much is Enough?

Long-term care (LTC) insurance is designed to cover the costs of personal care when you are unable to perform basic activities of daily living (ADLs) due to age, illness, or disability. These activities typically include bathing, dressing, eating, toileting, and mobility. Since Medicare and standard health insurance plans generally do not cover long-term care, having an LTC policy can provide financial protection and ease the burden of care costs, which can be overwhelming for both individuals and their families.

The amount of long-term care insurance you need depends on several factors, including your age, health, family medical history, and the type of care you may require in the future. Here's how to determine how much long-term care insurance is enough:

1. Assessing Your Risk of Needing Long-Term Care

Long-term care needs are typically associated with aging, though disabilities and chronic illnesses can also necessitate care at any age. The following considerations can help guide your decision:

- **Age:** The older you are, the higher your risk of needing long-term care. Most people who require LTC are in their 70s or older, but if you have a family history of certain diseases (e.g., Alzheimer's, Parkinson's), your risk may be higher.
- **Health and Family Medical History:** If you have pre-existing health conditions or a family history of chronic illnesses, you may be at greater risk of needing long-term care.

- **Gender:** Women, on average, live longer than men and are more likely to require long-term care. As a result, women typically need larger LTC policies than men.
- **Lifestyle:** Your lifestyle choices (e.g., regular exercise, diet, and preventive health measures) can influence your health and ability to avoid needing long-term care.

2. Determining the Level of Coverage

The level of long-term care insurance needed depends on the anticipated costs of care and your preferences regarding care options. Here's what to consider when determining coverage levels:

- **Daily Benefit Amount (DBA):** The DBA refers to the amount the policy will pay per day for your care. When selecting this amount, consider the average cost of care in your area. The average daily cost for nursing home care in the U.S. is around $250-$350, depending on location, while in-home care may cost between $150-$300 per day. Choose a DBA that can cover these costs or more, to ensure you have adequate financial protection. A good rule of thumb is to select a daily benefit amount that can cover the current cost of care, with room for future inflation. Policies with inflation protection can help ensure that your coverage keeps pace with rising costs.
- **Benefit Period:** This refers to the length of time the policy will pay for care. Most long-term care insurance policies offer benefit periods ranging from 2 years to a lifetime. Longer benefit periods are generally better because they ensure that coverage will last longer if your care needs are prolonged.

Common options:

- **2-5 years:** This is often a good starting point for those who want affordable premiums but still want to cover a significant period of care.
- **Lifetime coverage:** Ideal for those who want the peace of mind that they will be covered no matter how long they need care, but this will come with higher premiums.

- **Elimination Period (Waiting Period):** This is the number of days you must pay for long-term care out of pocket before your insurance policy begins to cover costs. Most policies have elimination periods ranging from 30 to 90 days. Shorter elimination periods will increase your premiums, so you must balance your ability to cover the waiting period with your long-term care budget.

Many people select an elimination period of 60-90 days, as this allows for a reasonable waiting period without significantly impacting the affordability of the policy.

3. Cost of Long-Term Care Insurance

Long-term care insurance premiums can vary widely based on factors such as your age, health, and the level of coverage you choose. However, there are some general guidelines to help estimate the cost:

- **Age at Purchase:** The younger you are when you buy LTC insurance, the lower your premiums will be. If you purchase a policy in your 40s or 50s, premiums can be relatively affordable. Premiums tend to increase as you age, so purchasing early can save you money in the long term.

For example, a healthy 50-year-old may pay around $1,500-$2,500 annually for a policy that covers a daily benefit of $200, a 3-year benefit period, and a 90-day elimination period. If you wait until you're 60 or older, the cost could rise significantly, potentially reaching $4,000 or more annually.

- **Customization:** LTC insurance policies are highly customizable, and you can adjust your coverage based on your budget. However, you should aim for enough coverage to prevent draining your savings if long-term care becomes necessary. If premiums are a concern, consider buying a policy with lower benefits or a longer elimination period.

4. Choosing Inflation Protection

One of the most important considerations when buying long-term care insurance is inflation protection. Healthcare costs, particularly long-term care, tend to rise faster than general inflation. Without inflation protection, the benefits of your policy may not be enough to cover future care needs.

Most policies offer inflation protection options, such as:

- **Compound inflation protection:** This increases your daily benefit amount by a certain percentage (usually 3-5%) each year to keep up with inflation.
- **Simple inflation protection:** This increases your daily benefit by a fixed amount each year, usually at a lower rate than compound inflation protection.

Inflation protection may increase your premiums but is essential to ensuring that your coverage will be sufficient in the future.

5. How Much Coverage is Enough?

To determine how much long-term care insurance is enough, follow these steps:

- **Estimate the cost of care in your area:** Research the cost of nursing homes, assisted living, and in-home care where you live. Consider whether you want to stay at home (home care) or are open to facility-based care, as the costs differ significantly.
- **Decide on a daily benefit:** Look for a daily benefit amount that covers at least half of the cost of care. For example, if nursing home care costs $250 per day in your area, you should aim for a policy that covers at least $150-$200 per day, with inflation protection to cover future increases.
- **Benefit period:** A 3-5 year benefit period is generally sufficient for most people, but you may choose lifetime coverage if you have the financial resources to afford it.

- **Elimination period:** The elimination period typically ranges from 30 to 90 days. A 60-day elimination period is a common choice for many policyholders, but a 90-day elimination period may offer lower premiums.

6. Who Should Consider Long-Term Care Insurance?

Long-term care insurance is particularly beneficial for:

- **People with significant assets:** If you have substantial savings or assets, long-term care insurance can help preserve those assets by covering the costs of care.
- **Those without significant family support:** If you do not have family members who can provide informal care, LTC insurance can ensure that you receive the necessary professional care without burdening your loved ones.
- **People with a family history of chronic conditions:** If your family has a history of chronic illnesses, such as Alzheimer's or dementia, you may be more likely to need long-term care in the future.

Conclusion

Long-term care insurance is a critical component of a well-rounded insurance plan, especially as we age. The right amount of coverage depends on your personal circumstances, including your financial situation, health, and the level of care you anticipate needing. By carefully considering factors such as daily benefit amounts, benefit periods, elimination periods, and inflation protection, you can create a plan that ensures you receive the care you need without sacrificing your financial stability.

Whole Life Insurance vs. Annuity: Understanding the Differences and Benefits

When considering insurance options, two key products often come up: **whole life insurance** and **annuities**. Both are unique financial instruments that offer long-term benefits, but they serve different purposes in a financial plan. Let's break down the differences between whole life insurance and annuities, explore how they are being used today, and explain the tax benefits associated with each.

Whole Life Insurance

What is Whole Life Insurance?

Whole life insurance is a type of permanent life insurance that provides coverage for your entire life, as long as premiums are paid. Unlike term life insurance, which only covers you for a specific period (e.g., 10, 20, or 30 years), whole life insurance remains in force as long as you live. In addition to providing a death benefit to your beneficiaries, whole life insurance also has a **cash value** component that accumulates over time.

How Does Whole Life Insurance Work?

- **Premiums:** You pay regular premiums, which are typically higher than those of term life insurance, but these premiums remain fixed throughout your life.
- **Cash Value Accumulation:** A portion of the premiums you pay goes into a cash value account, which grows over time, generally at a fixed rate. The cash value is tax-deferred, meaning you do not pay taxes on the growth of this value until you withdraw it.
- **Loans and Withdrawals:** You can borrow against the cash value of your policy, typically at favorable interest rates. However, any outstanding loans or withdrawals will reduce the death benefit if not repaid.
- **Death Benefit:** The primary benefit of whole life insurance is the guaranteed death benefit, which will be paid to your beneficiaries upon your passing, tax-free.

Current Uses of Whole Life Insurance:

- **Estate Planning:** Whole life insurance is often used as a tool for estate planning. The death benefit can be used to cover estate taxes, ensuring that your heirs do not have to liquidate assets to pay for taxes. It can also provide liquidity to your estate.
- **Wealth Accumulation:** The cash value of whole life insurance grows tax-deferred, making it an attractive option for those looking to accumulate wealth over time in a tax-efficient way. The policyholder can access this cash value through loans or withdrawals.
- **Retirement Planning:** Some individuals use whole life insurance as part of their retirement strategy. The tax-deferred growth of the cash value, combined with the predictable death benefit, can serve as a financial safety net in retirement.

Tax Benefits of Whole Life Insurance:

1. **Tax-Deferred Growth:** The cash value inside a whole life insurance policy grows without being subject to income taxes during the accumulation phase. This allows the policyholder to accumulate wealth over time without the burden of annual tax obligations.
2. **Tax-Free Death Benefit:** The death benefit paid to beneficiaries is typically free from income taxes. This makes whole life insurance an attractive option for those wishing to leave a legacy or ensure their family's financial security after death.
3. **Loan Proceeds:** If you take a loan against your policy's cash value, the loan is generally not taxable as long as the policy remains in force. However, if you fail to repay the loan, the amount may be deducted from your death benefit or cash value.

Why Consider Whole Life Insurance?

- **Lifetime Coverage:** Unlike term life, which expires after a certain period, whole life provides lifetime coverage.

- **Savings Component:** The cash value can be an attractive feature, offering both a death benefit and a way to accumulate wealth.
- **Stability:** Fixed premiums and guaranteed death benefits provide stability and predictability, making it a safe option for risk-averse individuals.

Annuities

What is an Annuity?

An annuity is a financial product that involves a contract between an individual and an insurance company, where the individual makes either a lump-sum payment or a series of payments in exchange for periodic income payments that begin immediately or at some point in the future. Annuities are typically used for retirement planning and can offer a reliable income stream for a set period or for the rest of the individual's life.

How Does an Annuity Work?

- **Accumulation Phase:** In the initial phase, you make either a lump-sum payment or a series of contributions to the insurance company. The money grows over time, either based on a fixed interest rate or variable investment options, depending on the type of annuity.
- **Payout Phase:** After a predetermined time or when you reach a certain age, the annuity begins making regular payments to you. These payments can be structured in a variety of ways (e.g., fixed amount, inflation-adjusted, lifetime, or for a set number of years).
- **Types of Annuities:**
  - **Fixed Annuities:** Provide guaranteed payouts that do not change over time.
  - **Variable Annuities:** Payouts can fluctuate based on the performance of underlying investments.

- **Immediate Annuities:** Begin payouts immediately after a lump-sum payment.
- **Deferred Annuities:** Payments begin at a later date, typically after a period of accumulation.

Current Uses of Annuities:

- **Retirement Income:** Annuities are commonly used as a tool for ensuring that you have a steady income stream during retirement. With the increasing uncertainty around pension plans and the decline of traditional retirement savings, annuities offer a reliable source of income, particularly when you want to ensure that you do not outlive your savings.
- **Wealth Preservation:** Annuities can be used to protect a portion of your wealth while providing guaranteed returns. For those who want to minimize the risk of market fluctuations and ensure consistent returns, fixed or immediate annuities are popular choices.
- **Estate Planning:** Some types of annuities can be structured to pass on benefits to beneficiaries, either as a lump sum or as ongoing payments, providing financial support for heirs after death.

Tax Benefits of Annuities:

1. **Tax-Deferred Growth:** Like whole life insurance, annuities benefit from tax-deferred growth. This means that any interest or investment returns accumulated within the annuity are not subject to annual taxes. This can result in greater growth potential over time.
2. **Tax Treatment of Payouts:** When you begin receiving payments, the portion of the payment that represents a return of your principal is not taxed. However, the earnings portion of the payment is taxed as ordinary income. This can be beneficial for individuals in lower tax brackets during retirement.

3. **No Contribution Limits:** Unlike retirement accounts like IRAs or 401(k)s, annuities have no contribution limits, which makes them attractive for those who want to save additional amounts for retirement once they have maxed out other tax-advantaged accounts.

4. **Roth Annuities:** A Roth annuity is funded with after-tax dollars, but future payouts are tax-free, which can be a beneficial option for those who expect to be in a higher tax bracket during retirement.

Why Consider Annuities?

- **Guaranteed Income:** Annuities are an excellent way to secure a guaranteed income stream, especially for those concerned about outliving their savings.
- **No Contribution Limits:** Annuities do not have the contribution limits imposed on retirement accounts, allowing for greater flexibility in saving for retirement.
- **Tax Deferral:** The tax-deferred growth of annuities can be beneficial for individuals seeking to accumulate wealth without paying taxes on gains each year.
- **Customizable Options:** Annuities come with various options, such as inflation adjustments, survivor benefits, and income riders, to tailor the product to your specific needs.

Whole Life Insurance vs. Annuity: Which Should You Choose?

Whole life insurance and **annuities** serve different purposes, but both can be valuable tools in a comprehensive financial plan. Here's how to decide which might be right for you:

- **Choose Whole Life Insurance if:**
  - You want lifelong coverage with a guaranteed death benefit.
  - You are interested in building a savings component (cash value) in a tax-deferred manner.
  - You want to provide a legacy for your heirs or cover estate taxes.

- You need stability and predictable premiums.

- **Choose an Annuity if:**
  - You are seeking a reliable, guaranteed income stream for retirement.
  - You are concerned about outliving your savings and want the security of a predictable income.
  - You want to accumulate wealth on a tax-deferred basis without contribution limits.
  - You prefer a product that allows flexibility in payout options.

Conclusion

Both whole life insurance and annuities are valuable insurance options that offer unique benefits and can be crucial components of a comprehensive financial plan. Whole life insurance offers the dual benefit of lifelong coverage and a cash value accumulation feature, with favorable tax treatment. On the other hand, annuities are excellent tools for ensuring retirement income and offering tax-deferred growth on contributions. Both come with tax advantages and should be considered depending on your long-term financial goals, risk tolerance, and retirement planning needs. Consulting with a financial advisor can help you determine which option, or combination of options, best suits your overall financial strategy.

In addition to **whole life insurance** and **annuities**, several other **tax-deferred** insurance products can help individuals grow their wealth, reduce taxable income, and plan for the future. These products are designed to offer tax advantages, primarily allowing the accumulation of value or earnings without being subject to taxes until they are withdrawn or paid out. Here are a few other types of tax-deferred insurance products to consider:

1. Universal Life Insurance (UL)

What is it? Universal Life Insurance is a type of permanent life insurance that combines a death benefit with a flexible savings component. It provides lifetime coverage like whole life but offers more flexibility in terms of premiums, death benefits, and cash value accumulation.

Tax-Deferred Benefits:

- **Cash Value Growth:** The cash value of a UL policy grows on a tax-deferred basis, meaning you don't pay taxes on the growth until you withdraw it or take a loan against it.
- **Loans and Withdrawals:** You can borrow against the cash value of your UL policy, and these loans are typically not taxable as long as the policy remains in force. However, if the policy lapses or if the loan exceeds the cash value, the loan may become taxable.

Why Consider It? Universal life offers more flexibility than whole life insurance, allowing you to adjust premiums and death benefits as your needs change. The tax-deferred growth and the ability to access cash value through loans or withdrawals can be attractive for long-term wealth accumulation.

2. Variable Life Insurance (VLI)

What is it? Variable Life Insurance is another form of permanent life insurance that combines a death benefit with an investment component. The cash value in a variable life policy can be allocated to various investment options, including stocks, bonds, or mutual funds.

Tax-Deferred Benefits:

- **Investment Growth:** The cash value grows on a tax-deferred basis, meaning any investment gains within the policy are not subject to income taxes until you withdraw them.
- **Tax-Free Loans:** As with other types of permanent life insurance, you can take loans against the cash value, which are generally not taxable as long as the policy remains in force.

Why Consider It? Variable life insurance offers the potential for higher returns compared to whole life or universal life, as the cash value is tied to the performance of chosen investments. However, this also introduces greater risk, and the value of your policy can fluctuate depending on market performance. It's best suited for those who want more control over their investments and are comfortable with market volatility.

3. Indexed Universal Life Insurance (IUL)

What is it? Indexed Universal Life Insurance is a form of universal life insurance where the cash value is tied to a stock market index (e.g., the S&P 500). While the cash value is not directly invested in the market, it's credited based on the index's performance, subject to a cap and a floor.

Tax-Deferred Benefits:

- **Tax-Deferred Growth:** The cash value grows on a tax-deferred basis, and the returns are linked to the performance of a market index, allowing for potential growth with less risk than variable life insurance.
- **Loan Options:** Like other permanent life policies, you can take loans against the cash value, and they are generally not taxable unless the policy lapses or loans exceed the cash value.

Why Consider It? IUL policies offer the upside potential of stock market growth while providing protection against market losses through a guaranteed floor (typically 0%). They offer a good balance between risk and reward, making them appealing to those looking for growth potential without the risks of direct stock market investment.

4. Deferred Compensation Plans (Non-Qualified Plans)

What are they? A **deferred compensation plan** is an arrangement between an employer and employee to defer a portion of the employee's income to a later date, typically at retirement. These plans are often structured to be funded through life insurance products, like **whole life**, **universal life**, or **variable life** policies.

Tax-Deferred Benefits:

- **Deferred Taxes:** The income or compensation deferred into these plans is not taxed until it's paid out, usually at retirement. Life insurance is used within these plans to provide death benefits and accumulate value that grows tax-deferred.
- **Flexible Payout Options:** The deferred income is often paid out as a lump sum or in periodic payments, potentially at a lower tax bracket during retirement.

Why Consider It? These plans are particularly useful for highly compensated employees, business owners, or executives looking for supplemental retirement income and additional life insurance benefits. They allow tax-deferred growth and provide a way to accumulate wealth outside of traditional retirement accounts.

5. Cash Value Life Insurance in Retirement Plans (e.g., 401(k) or IRA)

What is it? Some retirement plans, such as 401(k)s or IRAs, allow individuals to purchase life insurance within their retirement accounts. The policy can be used to provide death benefits as well as accumulate a cash value component.

Tax-Deferred Benefits:

- **Tax-Deferred Accumulation:** The cash value within the policy grows tax-deferred, and there's typically no tax liability until the cash value is withdrawn or the policy is cashed in.
- **Tax-Free Death Benefit:** The death benefit is paid to beneficiaries tax-free.

Why Consider It? While this strategy is not as common as traditional 401(k) or IRA contributions, it can be a useful option for those who are already maxing out their retirement contributions and are looking for additional ways to accumulate wealth in a tax-advantaged way.

6. Tax-Deferred Variable Universal Life Insurance (VUL)

What is it? Tax-deferred variable universal life insurance combines the flexibility of universal life insurance with the investment options of variable life insurance. The policyholder can choose to allocate the cash value among various investment options, and the growth is tied to those investments.

Tax-Deferred Benefits:

- **Tax-Deferred Investment Growth:** Similar to other variable life policies, the cash value in a VUL grows tax-deferred, and you do not pay taxes on gains until you withdraw the funds.
- **Tax-Free Loans:** Loans taken against the policy's cash value are generally tax-free, as long as the policy is active and the loan doesn't exceed the cash value.

Why Consider It? VUL policies are ideal for individuals who want both life insurance protection and the flexibility to manage their investments actively. However, they are best suited for those who are comfortable with investment risk, as the cash value can fluctuate based on market performance.

7. Flexible Premium Life Insurance

What is it? Flexible premium life insurance refers to policies where you can adjust the premiums you pay based on your financial situation. These policies allow you to pay higher premiums when you can afford to, which can increase your cash value, or lower them when needed, as long as the policy remains in force.

Tax-Deferred Benefits:

- **Tax-Deferred Cash Value Growth:** Just like other permanent life insurance policies, the cash value in a flexible premium policy grows tax-deferred. You can also take loans or withdrawals against the cash value on a tax-deferred basis.

- **Tax-Free Death Benefit:** The death benefit is typically tax-free to beneficiaries.

Why Consider It? This product is attractive to those looking for more flexibility in managing life insurance premiums and cash value accumulation. It offers the potential for tax-deferred growth and allows individuals to tailor the policy to their current financial circumstances.

Conclusion

Besides **whole life** and **annuities**, several other **tax-deferred insurance products** can play vital roles in financial planning and wealth accumulation. **Universal life**, **variable life**, **indexed universal life**, **deferred compensation plans**, and other flexible insurance options all offer tax advantages, with the potential for growth and financial protection. The common thread across all these products is their ability to accumulate cash value on a **tax-deferred** basis, providing individuals with tax-efficient ways to build wealth and plan for retirement while also offering life insurance protection.

When choosing a tax-deferred insurance product, it's important to consider your financial goals, risk tolerance, and whether you are looking for flexibility or a more structured approach. Consulting with a financial advisor can help you determine the best products for your unique situation.

How to Shop for Insurance: A Step-by-Step Guide

Shopping for insurance can feel overwhelming, especially with the variety of options available for life, health, auto, home, and other types of coverage. However, it's an essential task to ensure that you are adequately protected and not overpaying. To help simplify the process, here's a step-by-step guide on how to shop for insurance effectively.

Step 1: Understand Your Insurance Needs

Before you start shopping for insurance, you need to clearly understand what you need. Different types of insurance serve various purposes, so it's crucial to know what coverage is necessary for your life, property, and health.

- **Assess Your Situation:** Are you shopping for life insurance, health insurance, auto insurance, or home insurance? The type of coverage you need will dictate the specifics of your search.
- **Identify Risks:** What risks do you face? For example, if you own a home, home insurance might be essential. If you're the primary breadwinner in your family, life insurance may be necessary. If you drive a car, auto insurance is required by law in most states.
- **Understand Minimum Requirements:** Some types of insurance, such as auto or home insurance, have minimum coverage limits required by law. Be sure to understand these to avoid legal or financial trouble.

Step 2: Determine Your Budget

Insurance premiums vary widely depending on factors like your age, location, health status, type of coverage, and the insurance company you choose. Knowing your budget helps narrow down options.

- **Evaluate Your Finances:** Take a close look at your budget and determine how much you can afford to spend on insurance each month. Remember, while it might be tempting to go for the cheapest option, the lowest premium may not always provide adequate coverage.
- **Factor in Deductibles and Co-pays:** In addition to monthly premiums, consider any deductibles (the amount you pay out-of-pocket before insurance kicks in) and co-pays (shared costs between you and the insurer). These factors impact your total financial responsibility.

Step 3: Research Insurance Companies and Products

Once you know your needs and budget, start researching the different insurance products available. Look at various insurance companies and the coverage they offer.

- **Online Comparison Tools:** Use websites that allow you to compare quotes from different insurance companies. These tools can help you quickly gather options and compare them.

- **Check Financial Strength:** Ensure the company you are considering has strong financial stability. You can review ratings from agencies like A.M. Best, Standard & Poor's, or Moody's to see how financially secure the insurer is.

- **Review Coverage Options:** Review policy types, coverage limits, exclusions, and the amount of customer service each company provides. Make sure to compare the details of each product to ensure you're not overpaying for something you don't need or missing out on necessary coverage.

Step 4: Request Quotes and Compare

Once you've narrowed down the insurers you're considering, request quotes from multiple companies. Most insurers offer online quote generators, but you can also call agents to get a personalized quote.

- **Provide Accurate Information:** To receive an accurate quote, provide the insurance company with accurate details, such as your age, location, health status, and other relevant factors. A discrepancy in information can result in higher premiums or inadequate coverage.

- **Compare Policies Side by Side:** Look at the premiums, coverage limits, deductibles, exclusions, and customer service reviews of each quote. Compare similar policies to find the best balance between cost and coverage.

- **Ask About Discounts:** Inquire about available discounts, such as bundling multiple policies (e.g., combining auto and home insurance), maintaining a safe driving record, or having a good credit score. Some insurers offer discounts for things like having a home security system or being a non-smoker.

Step 5: Understand the Policy Terms and Conditions

Once you've received your quotes, don't rush to make a decision without fully understanding the details of each policy. Carefully review the terms and conditions of each option.

- **Read the Fine Print:** Look out for exclusions, such as specific conditions or situations not covered by the insurance, as well as the fine print on policy renewals and premium increases. Ensure that the policy provides the level of protection you need.
- **Clarify Ambiguities:** If there's anything you don't understand in the policy or quote, ask the insurer for clarification. It's better to ask questions up front than deal with unexpected coverage gaps later.
- **Check for Riders:** Some policies offer optional riders that can add extra coverage. For example, in life insurance, you might opt for a "waiver of premium" rider if you're unable to work due to illness or disability. In home insurance, you may want additional coverage for valuables like jewelry or artwork.

Step 6: Review Customer Service and Claims Process

Insurance is more than just about paying premiums; it's about ensuring you're supported when you need help. Customer service and claims handling are essential factors to consider.

- **Customer Reviews:** Look at online reviews and ratings from other customers to understand how the insurance company handles claims and customer service. Customer feedback can provide valuable insight into the company's responsiveness and reliability.

- **Claims Process:** Research how the company handles claims. A good insurer should have a simple, clear, and fast claims process. Check if they offer 24/7 claims support and if their claims processing times are reasonable.

- **Ask for Recommendations:** If you know someone who has insurance with the company you're considering, ask them about their experiences. Word-of-mouth recommendations are often more reliable than online reviews.

Step 7: Finalize Your Purchase

After carefully reviewing all your options, it's time to finalize your purchase.

- **Check Your Payment Schedule:** Choose a payment schedule (monthly, quarterly, or annually) that works best for your budget. Some insurance companies offer discounts for paying annually instead of monthly.

- **Read the Policy Again:** Before you sign, carefully review the finalized policy to ensure all the details match what you were quoted, including premiums, coverage limits, and exclusions.

- **Ensure Your Coverage Is Effective:** Verify the start date of the policy to ensure you're properly covered as soon as possible.

Step 8: Keep Your Insurance Policy Up to Date

Once you've purchased insurance, remember that life circumstances change. It's important to periodically review and update your insurance policies to ensure they still meet your needs.

- **Life Changes:** Major life events, such as marriage, the birth of a child, purchasing a home, or retiring, may require changes to your coverage.

- **Regular Reviews:** Review your insurance policies every year or whenever a significant change occurs in your life. Keep in mind that some insurers offer annual renewals, which may include premium adjustments.

Conclusion

Shopping for insurance can seem complex, but breaking it down into manageable steps makes the process more straightforward. Start by understanding your needs, setting a budget, and researching insurance companies. Gather quotes, compare policies, and understand the details of each option before making your decision. By taking the time to shop around, ask questions, and review the fine print, you can make an informed decision and find the best insurance coverage for your specific needs. Always keep your policy up to date to ensure you're continuously protected as your life evolves.

Chapter 11

Final Chapter: The Path Forward: Empowering Your Financial Journey

As you turn to the last page of this book, remember that the journey toward financial empowerment is an ongoing process, one that requires intention, reflection, and action. The knowledge you've gained from these chapters isn't meant to be a destination but a roadmap to guide you through the intricate landscape of personal finance. Whether you're a woman just beginning to navigate your financial path or someone well on her way, the principles outlined here can serve as a foundation for building a secure, prosperous future.

The Power of Knowledge

At the core of financial independence lies knowledge. By reading this book, you've taken the first step in understanding the intricacies of financial planning, investing, tax strategies, and retirement planning. Knowledge is a powerful tool—it empowers you to make informed decisions that can affect your present and future well-being. Remember, financial literacy isn't about having all the answers immediately; it's about developing a mindset of continuous learning and curiosity.

The next step is applying what you've learned. Financial decisions should be made thoughtfully, with an understanding of both the short-term and long-term implications. By applying the concepts of budgeting, investing, and planning to your life, you'll gradually see the transformation of your financial situation from one of uncertainty to one of control.

A Holistic Approach to Financial Planning

Financial planning is never a one-size-fits-all endeavor. Each of us has unique needs, desires, and circumstances. Your financial journey is deeply personal, shaped by your values, goals, and priorities. Therefore, it's important to approach your financial plan holistically—considering not only your immediate financial needs but also your long-term aspirations. Whether that means ensuring a comfortable retirement, funding your children's education, or creating a legacy for future generations, your financial plan should align with your unique vision.

As women, we often wear many hats—daughter, sister, partner, mother, and professional. It's essential to design a financial strategy that fits your lifestyle and supports your goals. This may involve seeking advice from trusted professionals, such as financial advisors, tax experts, or insurance specialists. Never underestimate the importance of a support network to guide you through complex financial decisions.

The Importance of Building a Team of Experts

While you may feel capable of handling some aspects of your financial planning on your own, the complexity of certain financial decisions often requires expert advice. This is where building a trusted team comes into play. Consider financial advisors who specialize in women's wealth, tax professionals who can help you navigate tax strategies, and insurance experts who can ensure you're adequately protected.

When selecting these professionals, look for individuals who understand your goals and are committed to helping you achieve them. Look for advisors who can guide you in making decisions that benefit both your immediate needs and long-term financial health. The right advisors can make a significant difference in how efficiently you reach your financial milestones.

Taking Action and Staying Consistent

Financial empowerment is not a passive endeavor—it requires consistent action. You must be proactive in managing your money, keeping track of your spending, saving diligently, and investing wisely. As you continue to implement the strategies you've learned in this book, stay consistent and patient with your efforts. Financial success doesn't happen overnight, but with disciplined planning and commitment, you'll see the results over time.

It's also important to periodically review your financial plan. Life events such as a job change, marriage, divorce, or the birth of a child can significantly impact your financial situation. By revisiting your plan regularly, you can ensure that your financial strategy evolves as your circumstances change. Flexibility is key in ensuring long-term financial success.

Your Financial Future

The road to financial independence is paved with both challenges and triumphs, but you don't have to walk it alone. Whether you're planning for retirement, building an emergency fund, or exploring investment opportunities, remember that you have the tools and knowledge to create a secure and prosperous financial future. The ultimate goal is not just financial stability, but the freedom to live your life on your own terms.

This book has given you the framework to begin that journey. Now, it's up to you to take the next steps—armed with knowledge, confidence, and the support of experts when needed. Your financial journey will continue to evolve, but with each step you take, you'll become more empowered to make decisions that serve your best interests.

As you close this book, remember that the path to financial empowerment is within your reach. You are capable of taking charge of your financial future, and with the right tools, resources, and mindset, you can achieve financial independence. Your financial journey is unique, and there's no better time than now to begin crafting the future you desire.

Take a deep breath, trust in your ability, and step confidently onto the path of financial empowerment. You've got this!

Thank you for trusting me to guide you through this journey. I wish you success, peace, and financial freedom as you move forward.

www.ingramcontent.com/pod-product-compliance
Lightning Source LLC
LaVergne TN
LVHW062148200926
848484LV00007B/1883